By His Wounds You Are Healed

how the message of Ephesians

transforms a woman's identity

Wendy Horger Alsup

Special thanks to my pastor, John Haralson, and his wife Linn for teaching me from the pulpit and then living out practically before me the true meaning of gospel grace. The gospel really does change everything, and I understand now more than ever what that means.

Contents

Introduction

Who are you? How do you describe yourself to others? For what do you want to be known? And in the stillness when no one else is around, how do you view yourself? If you are like me, you have likely spent much of your life trying to figure out who you are and what purposes and accomplishments will give meaning to your life. Since I was a young child, I have watched others' responses to things I said and did. Longing for affirmation and approval, their reactions determined how I would act next. As I grew up, I admired from afar those who seemed comfortable in their own skin with the confidence to *act* as they were convicted rather than *react* in light of others' actions toward them. Nowhere was this more obvious than my years of middle and high school. I was classically insecure—constantly tweaking my appearance and personality to conform to the popular people—then withdrawing altogether when I could not figure out the magic formula for changing my image with either my peers or myself.

The problem was that I was trying to conform to the wrong image. You will see this clearly if you read farther into this study of Ephesians with me. This was highlighted to me as I prepared for my 20th high school reunion.   Despite all the life-lessons learned and maturity gained in the last two decades, I found myself falling back into the same old patterns of insecure thinking as I contemplated what it would take to make me walk confidently back into the small town country club where I experienced my last painful high school dance. I joined a gym months in advance so I could lose the baby fat that clung to me two years after the birth of my son. If I was going to return to the scene of the crime, I wanted to be svelte when I did so. But after five months of faithful exercise, I had not lost a pound. I searched dress stores for the perfect outfit that would reflect the perfect image—to no avail. My husband finally told me to just be myself and wear the kind of clothes that I normally wear. That really scared me. Wear my usual style of clothes? Do not try to project something about myself that is not true? But that leaves me exposed! I am a bit heavy and most comfortable in jeans and a black shirt. Who I am going to impress that way?

I started to listen to myself. I sounded like an insecure teenager trying to determine her outfit for her senior prom. Was I really that dependent on my DRESS to prop me up to meet these people I had not seen in twenty years? Did I not have anything better than that on which to rely?

During that season of contemplating my high school reunion, I also began a study of Ephesians. There is a sense in which Ephesians is a condensed version of the whole story of Scripture. I had read through it before and heard several sermon series on it as well. But this time was different. This time, I was aware of my insecurities in a way I had not been before, and I was deeply moved by what I read. Ephesians defines my identity and security in Christ. It tells me in detail of the real benefits I have as a daughter of God. It shows me how these benefits equip me to reclaim my identity in Christ. And it draws a straight line from all those gospel truths to the heart of my insecurities today. It shows me how to walk into my 20th class reunion as a secure woman who knows who she is in Jesus.

Equipping me to face the mental battles attached to my class reunion is just one small way the good news of Ephesians has impacted me. I will share more ways this study has challenged and encouraged me as we go forward. But what about you? Back to the opening question of this book, who are YOU? What triggers your insecurities? To what do you look to define your worth and establish your identity? Is it your degree or career? Did the bottom drop out from under you when you lost your high-status job in your field of choice? Is it your husband? Does your daily happiness depend on his affirmation and approval of you? Is it your children? Do you feel pride over their successes and shame over their failures? They have the power to tear your heart out, you know. Raising my children has exposed my insecurities at an entirely new level. Or if you do not have a husband or children, do you feel like you are in a holding pattern with no personal identity until God gives them to you? To what are you looking for your identity and security? I believe that you, like me, will find answers in Ephesians to these questions that will sustain you for a lifetime.

As you begin reading this concise discussion of the message of Ephesians to women, you might wonder two things. First, why have a book on Ephesians written specifically to women, and second, why does the title of this book come not from Ephesians but from the Old Testament? I will answer the second question first. In Isaiah 53:5, the prophet Isaiah gives an intriguing prophecy of the coming Messiah that sets us up well for the message of Ephesians.

> But he was pierced for our transgressions,
> he was crushed for our iniquities;
> the punishment that brought us peace was upon him,
> and by his wounds we are healed.

We know this Messiah to be Jesus and this promise to be fulfilled on the cross. Isaiah's prophecy was that the Messiah's punishment on the cross would buy us our peace and that the wounds he endured on the cross would purchase our healing. What do you think of this prophecy? Is this only a feel good saying that we hope one day becomes reality? Or do we believe this is true for us today? Do you and I walk daily believing that his punishment on the cross has bought OUR peace, and by his wounds WE are healed? And do we even know what the words peace and healing mean for us?

If you have been around Christians for any length of time, you know that many of us acknowledge the good news of the gospel but often walk around in tragic hopelessness despite it all. We can quote the gospel, but we have not experienced the full transformation it provides. We know it, but we do not always use it. We talk about it, but we often do not apply it. When issues heat up our lives, we see the areas in which we need to appropriate to our benefit all Christ has purchased for us on the cross.

A friend recently recounted to me the story of Hetty Green, known as the Wicked Witch of Wall Street in the early part of the last century. The story goes that she took so long trying to find a free clinic to treat her son's broken leg that he had to have it amputated after it got gangrene. Yet, she was born into a wealthy family and died with a net worth of hundreds of millions of dollars. My friend summed up Green's life with the statement, "She never tapped into her wealth."

Friends, that is the spiritual state of many of us. We have a spiritual inheritance of infinite worth in the here and now, and we need to avail ourselves of our spiritual wealth. Christ has accomplished something deep and transforming for you personally on the cross, and the benefits to you of being rooted in him are beyond your ability to fully conceive—but you need to try! When you wrestle to understand the fullness of what you have IN HIM, it transforms your life, your church, and your relationships. It equips you to quench all the fiery darts of the enemy. This is the message of Ephesians. By his wounds, you are healed.

Is this healing just for women? Certainly not! If the message of Ephesians is not just for women, then why limit the scope of this book this way? For a long time, I have been burdened that most Bible commentaries and books on Bible doctrine are written by men and aimed at a mostly male audience. My experience is that many women skip these books and focus instead on books on women's topics by women authors. As I have studied through Ephesians, I have been strongly convicted that the content of the book is essential for me as a woman—as a wife, a mom, a sister, a daughter, a friend, a neighbor, and a coworker. My hope is that this study by a female author with mostly feminine applications will encourage more women to take the book of Ephesians seriously for themselves.

This book is not an exhaustive look at Paul's letter to the Ephesian believers. Martin Lloyd Jones wrote an eight-volume commentary on Ephesians, and some may argue that he missed some points. This short study is simply a survey of the book. I am not consistent in how much information I present on each verse, chapter, or section. Some chapters are short. Some are long. Some verses are skipped, while others may have two chapters dedicated to them. The purpose of this book was not to focus on minute detail but rather to clearly articulate the coherent, connected message Paul presents throughout the letter. The content of each chapter is geared to fit that goal rather than to study exhaustively the meaning of each individual phrase.

There is room at the end of most chapters to write out your reflections on what you read. The words of Ephesians are written out again and again because the Scripture itself is much more important than my commentary on it. Interact with the Scripture. Mark it up. Circle words. Highlight phrases. Do whatever helps you internalize the message of Ephesians for yourself. If room to write in this text is helpful to you, please make use of it. However, not everyone will want to make notes, scribble ideas, or write out their thoughts. It this format does not fit your learning style, feel free to ignore these aspects of the study. The same applies to the discussion questions at the end.

In my study of Ephesians, *The Message of Ephesians* commentary by John Stott has been an invaluable resource. Listen to Stott's overview of the book of Ephesians:

> It tells how Jesus Christ shed his blood in a sacrificial death for sin, was then raised from death by the power of God, and has been exalted above all competitors to the supreme place in both the universe and the church. More than that, we who are 'in Christ', organically united to him by faith, have ourselves shared in these great events. We have been raised from spiritual death, exalted to heaven and seated with him there. We have also been reconciled to God and to each

other. As a result, through Christ and in Christ, we are nothing less than God's new society, the single new humanity which he is creating and which includes Jews and Gentiles on equal terms. We are the family of God the Father, the body of Jesus Christ his Son, and the temple or dwelling place of the Holy Spirit.

Therefore we are to demonstrate plainly and visibly by our new life the reality of this new thing which God has done: first by the unity and diversity of our common life, secondly by the purity and love of our everyday behavior, next by the mutual submissiveness and care of our relationships at home, and lastly by our stability in the fight against the principalities and powers of evil. Then in the fullness of time God's purpose of unification will be brought to completion under the headship of Jesus Christ. ... The whole letter is thus a magnificent combination of Christian doctrine and Christian duty, Christian faith and Christian life, what God has done through Christ and what we must be and do in consequence.[1]

I hope Stott's summary encourages you to stick with this study as we unpack the message of Ephesians. Notice his emphasis on the interplay of "Christian faith and Christian life." The connection of these two parts of our lives is essential to the message of Ephesians. Ephesians describes the essence of what it means to be a Christian—a very theological beginning (faith) that works itself out in very practical ways (life). Our belief system and our daily lives are intimately connected. Ephesians does not just tell us they are connected, but it shows us clearly how the one affects the other. It does not start with moral standards that you obey that God would bless you. The message of Ephesians is in fact the exact opposite. The Apostle Paul is intent that we understand the blessings that have been eternally secured for us by Christ despite our unworthiness, and from understanding those unconditional blessings, we then learn obedience.

As we read through the book of Ephesians and discuss each section, my goal is to continually bring the content of the book back to this foundational question, "How does this teaching impact me right now?" Paul is going to teach us thoroughly about the behind-the-scenes spiritual work Christ has accomplished and is continuing to accomplish for us. Then Paul teaches us what that means for our relationships with other believers, with our parents, in our marriages, with our children, in oppressive work environments, and in every spiritual attack Satan sends our way.

I have many spiritual faults, but I like to think that hypocrisy is not one of them (perhaps I am self-deluded). As I thought about putting these words on paper, it was obvious to me that I had to wrestle with this in my own daily routine before I could exhort anyone else. For me, the current daily issue was not a horrible, big, overwhelming thing. Rather, my struggle was more like a leaky, dripping faucet. My young son who would not stay in his own bed woke me out of a deep sleep several times in the early morning. While certainly not the worst of circumstances, it started my day down a negative trajectory that had me gritting my teeth not to scream in frustration at everyone around me in my house. I realized quickly my need to deal with God. "God, I know from Ephesians that you have accomplished something on the cross that is supposed to transform how I handle these situations. What do I have in Christ? What does it mean to be conformed to his image? How does that look right now? God, enlighten me. I need to understand the hope of what you called me to be, because I hate the way I am acting right now and do not want to be like

---

[1] John Stott, *The Message of Ephesians* (Downer's Grove, Ill: Intervarsity Press, 1979), 25.

this toward my husband and children." And God began to transform my thinking. He reminded me that Christ has made a way for me to no longer be controlled by my anger and frustration. He prompted me to ask forgiveness of my husband and children for my angry responses. In time, the hope according to Ephesians of what I have in Christ edged out the hopelessness I felt in my initial responses.

As we begin our look at Ephesians, I want to be clear upfront. This book is not about supernatural spiritual power to change your circumstances. This is not about single women suddenly finding godly spouses or barren women unexpectedly bearing twins. It is not about homeless couples winning the lottery or underappreciated employees seeing miraculous transformations in their oppressive jobs. *This is not about hope that our circumstances will change.* This is about hope that God has done something on the cross that changes how we think about our circumstances! This is about responding with grace when we used to choose anger. This is about learning to endure in peace when we used to fret with impatience. This is about getting a vision for what God has done and is continuing to do for us in the heavenly realm and letting that vision make a real, radical difference in how we approach our struggles daily.

By his wounds (not circumstantial change), we are healed.

Reflections

_____
_____
_____
_____
_____
_____
_____
_____
_____
_____
_____
_____
_____
_____
_____
_____
_____
_____
_____

Section 1 Ephesians 1:1-2:10

Written from prison around A. D. 60, Ephesians is unique among Paul's letters because he is not addressing a specific doctrinal or sin issue in the church there. Unlike 1 Corinthians in which some guy is sleeping with his step-mother or Galatians in which Peter is tolerating a legalistic view of the gospel, Paul gets to talk to the church at Ephesus about the big picture of the benefits of Christ's sacrifice for us on the cross and the way that impacts our entire lives. The book reflects a very connected, coherent thought process from beginning to end. Each thought builds succinctly on the previous thought, and context means everything in Ephesians. Unlike Proverbs, where you can pull two or three verses out and prepare an accurate, concise lesson from them, no piece of Ephesians can be pulled out and accurately handled without clearly examining the whole book.

The six chapters of Ephesians naturally break into four parts, each with a fairly consistent theme. Ephesians 1:1-2:10 sets up the theology of what Christ has accomplished for us on the cross and all the blessings we have spiritually in him. Then Ephesians 2:11-3:24 discusses how our reconciliation to Christ paves the way for our reconciliation to others, in particular reconciling the most historically divisive conflict in all of human history, that of the Jew and the Gentile. Ephesians 4:1-5:21 dives deeply into the practical implications of our oneness with Christ on our relationships with others in his Body, the Church. Finally, in Ephesians 5:22-6:24, Paul teaches how our reconciliation to God through Christ equips us to be reconciled with our spouses, children, and coworkers, empowering us to do battle with Satan in every way.

Of the four sections, this first one is the hardest to endure in my opinion. The truths presented here are deep, but they are also worth knowing. I hope you will persevere through them because getting this foundation is key to unlocking the very practical application Paul makes in the later sections.

Read through Ephesians 1:1 – 2:10. Note the words or phrases that stand out to you.

Ephesians 1

[1]Paul, an apostle of Christ Jesus by the will of God,

To the saints who are in Ephesus, and are faithful in Christ Jesus:
[2]Grace to you and peace from God our Father and the Lord Jesus Christ.

[3]Blessed be the God and Father of our Lord Jesus Christ, who has blessed us in Christ with every spiritual blessing in the heavenly places, [4]even as he chose us in him before the foundation of the world, that we should be holy and blameless before him. In love [5]he predestined us for adoption as sons through Jesus Christ, according to the purpose of his will, [6]to the praise of his glorious grace, with which he has blessed us in the Beloved. [7]In him we have redemption through his blood, the forgiveness of our trespasses, according to the riches of his grace, [8]which he lavished upon us, in all wisdom and insight [9]making known to us the mystery of his will, according to his purpose, which he set forth in Christ [10]as a plan for the fullness of time, to unite all things in him, things in heaven and things on earth.

[11]In him we have obtained an inheritance, having been predestined according to the purpose of him who works all things according to the counsel of his will, [12]so that we who were the first to hope in Christ might be to the praise of his glory. [13]In him you also, when you heard the word of truth, the gospel of your salvation, and believed in him, were sealed with the promised Holy Spirit, [14]who is the guarantee of our inheritance until we acquire possession of it, to the praise of his glory.

[15]For this reason, because I have heard of your faith in the Lord Jesus and your love toward all the saints, [16]I do not cease to give thanks for you, remembering you in my prayers, [17]that the God of our Lord Jesus Christ, the Father of glory, may give you a spirit of wisdom and of revelation in the knowledge of him, [18]having the eyes of your hearts enlightened, that you may know what is the hope to which he has called you, what are the riches of his glorious inheritance in the saints, [19]and what is the immeasurable greatness of his power toward us who believe, according to the working of his great might [20]that he worked in Christ when he raised him from the dead and seated him at his right hand in the heavenly places,

[21]far above all rule and authority and power and dominion, and above every name that is named, not only in this age but also in the one to come. [22]And he put all things under his feet and gave him as head over all things to the church, [23]which is his body, the fullness of him who fills all in all.

Ephesians 2

[1]And you were dead in the trespasses and sins [2]in which you once walked, following the course of this world, following the prince of the power of the air, the spirit that is now at work in the sons of disobedience— [3]among whom we all once lived in the passions of our flesh, carrying out the desires of the body and the mind, and were by nature children of wrath, like the rest of mankind. [4]But God, being rich in mercy, because of the great love with which he loved us, [5]even when we were dead in our trespasses, made us alive together with Christ— by grace you have been saved— [6]and raised us up with him and seated us with him in the heavenly places in Christ Jesus, [7]so that in the coming ages he might show the immeasurable riches of his grace in kindness toward us in Christ Jesus. [8]For by grace you have been saved through faith. And this is not your own doing; it is the gift of God, [9]not a result of works, so that no one may boast. [10]For we are his workmanship, created in Christ Jesus for good works, which God prepared beforehand, that we should walk in them.

Chapter 1 Ephesians 1: 1-2

We begin with the opening greeting by Paul to the believers in Ephesus.

1 Paul, an apostle of Christ Jesus by the will of God,
To the saints who are in Ephesus, and are faithful in Christ Jesus:
2 Grace to you and peace from God our Father and the Lord Jesus Christ.

In his commentary, John Stott points out that much of the message of Ephesians is summed up in the opening salutation, "Grace to you and peace from God our Father and the Lord Jesus Christ."[2]

Grace

The Greek word translated grace is *charis*.[3] It shows up 12 times in Ephesians, 18 times in II Corinthians, and 22 times in Romans. As I attempted to sum up the meaning of the term for this book, I was struck by the complexity of the ways it is used in Scripture. In short, it means loving-kindness, favor, or gift. But I am afraid those three words do not really plumb the depths of Paul's salutation of *grace* to the believers at Ephesus. As we get deeper into Ephesians 1 and 2, we will get an informed picture of the specifics of what God means when he uses the term *grace*. But for right now, let us at least understand the basics.

I looked up *grace* in Hebrew, Greek, and English dictionaries. Each gave really long definitions from multiple angles. But the common thread in each use of the term is that it is **not** about giving what is due. Consider these verses from the New Testament that use the same Greek word for grace, *charis*.

Romans 4:4 Now to the one who works, his wages are not counted as a *gift* but as his due.

Luke 6 32 If you love those who love you, what *benefit* is that to you? For even sinners love those who love them. 33 And if you do good to those who do good to you, what *benefit* is that to you? For even sinners do the same. 34 And if you lend to those from whom you expect to receive, what *credit* is that to you? Even sinners lend to sinners, to get back the same amount. 35 But love your enemies, and do good, and lend, expecting nothing in return, and your reward will be great, and you will be sons of the Most High, for he is kind to the ungrateful and the evil. 36 Be merciful, even as your Father is merciful.

When you give back what is earned or deserved, it is not *charis*—it is not grace. It is not favor or benefit, and it is not credited toward you as anything other than exactly what you are expected to do. Instead, grace does what is unexpected, undeserved, and out of line with reasonable

---

[2] Stott, p. 27.
[3] James Strong, *The New Strong's Exhaustive Concordance of the Bible* (Nashville: Thomas Nelson, 1990), s. v. "charis."

responses. Grace is an unreasonable response—unreasonably good, but unreasonable nonetheless. When we give grace, this undeserved favor that does good to enemies and lends expecting nothing in return, then we give evidence of our relationship with our Father in heaven, because this is his calling card. He is kind to the ungrateful and evil. He is full of grace.

Grace is fundamental to the rest of the message of Ephesians. It is possibly one of the most often used but least understood words in Christian circles. I learned the acronym for grace, "God's riches at Christ's expense," in Sunday school as a child. But I did not understand grace. I understood that I did not earn my salvation, but my response was to start trying to earn it from that point forward. If God was that good to me, then I needed to start being a better person so that I could pay him back a bit. But Jesus in Luke 6 sets a different criteria altogether as evidence of our understanding of grace. Jesus says the evidence of our understanding of God's grace toward us is **our grace toward others**.

Grace and humility are intertwined theological concepts. When we get grace, the only choice is humility. In Christian circles, we sometimes mistake other virtues for grace and humility. I know Christian leaders who are diplomatic, generally friendly, or polite. But these traits are not the same as grace and the humility that follows it. Grace is an unreasonably lavish response to those undeserving of it, based on our own understanding of God's great, undeserved favor toward us. As we go forward, we need to examine ourselves to make sure we do not mistake our politeness or good manners for this altogether different thing named grace to which God has called us.

Peace

Here is a word that grabs my attention. I long for peace—peace from war, peace in my racially diverse community, peace in my family, and peace between Christian brothers and sisters who bite and devour each other when they should be each other's best advocates. When the Apostle Paul mentions the word peace, my ears perk up immediately. I want this! How? Where? When? I am sick of strife and conflict! Please, give me the key to unlocking the gift of peace for me, my family, my church, and my community. Once again, we are too early in our look at Ephesians to unpack all to which Paul is referring here. But, to whet your appetite, here is the definition of the Greek word translated as peace—"exemption from the rage and havoc of war, peace between individuals, harmony, concord, security, safety, prosperity, felicity, (because peace and harmony make and keep things safe and prosperous)... the tranquil state of a soul assured of its salvation through Christ, and so fearing nothing from God and content with its earthly lot, of whatsoever sort that is."[4]

We are talking about *peace through grace*. Do you want that? Does that phrase evoke hope in you for the future? To be clear, both Paul's and Jesus' examples teach us this is not peace FROM trials, but peace THROUGH trials, and it is found by understanding and applying God's free grace.

As I was writing the first draft of this manuscript, I initially included only one paragraph on the concept of grace. Then God brought me through some personal experiences that opened my eyes to my own lack of understanding of grace, after which I wrote a few more paragraphs as I studied it more in Scripture. But that was not enough. A few weeks later I got full-fledged writer's block.

---

[4] Strongs, s. v. "eirene."

Or maybe more accurately, God stopped me from writing another word. For the next few months, I could not compose anything for this manuscript as God bombarded me with situations that revealed to me my own limited understanding of God's grace. It became obvious to me that grace is more than just a relatively important Christian principle. It is the CORE VALUE of the gospel.

I knew that conflict kills—it kills relationships, it kills joy, and it kills momentum in the work of God. I believed that Stott's summary phrase of Ephesians, *peace through grace,* was accurate. But I did not understand it at a soul-deep level. Over the months of writer's block, the depth of my need of God's grace and his demand that I extend it to others finally sunk in. I hate conflict. I want peace. But peace is only possible through a full, rich, deep understanding of the grace, love, and forgiveness that God has shown us and the grace, love, and forgiveness he demands of us in response toward others. Keep the summary statement, *peace through grace,* in mind as we travel deeper into Ephesians. It is a phrase of utmost importance as we move forward.

Now onto verses 3- 14.

Reflections

God himself choose us for himself. Before the plan of the world — and wants to grant us every blessing w/ unmerited favor that begins w/ his grace + peace. God consummated his blessing to us by the gift of the Holy Spirit. And grant us wisdom and insight w/ his glorious favor.

Chapter 2 Ephesians 1:3-14

3 Blessed be the God and Father of our Lord Jesus Christ, who has blessed us in Christ with every spiritual blessing in the heavenly places, 4 even as he chose us in him before the foundation of the world, that we should be holy and blameless before him. In love 5 he predestined us for adoption as sons through Jesus Christ, according to the purpose of his will, 6 to the praise of his glorious grace, with which he has blessed us in the Beloved. 7 In him we have redemption through his blood, the forgiveness of our trespasses, according to the riches of his grace, 8 which he lavished upon us, in all wisdom and insight 9 making known to us the mystery of his will, according to his purpose, which he set forth in Christ 10 as a plan for the fullness of time, to unite all things in him, things in heaven and things on earth.

11 In him we have obtained an inheritance, having been predestined according to the purpose of him who works all things according to the counsel of his will, 12 so that we who were the first to hope in Christ might be to the praise of his glory. 13 In him you also, when you heard the word of truth, the gospel of your salvation, and believed in him, were sealed with the promised Holy Spirit, 14 who is the guarantee of our inheritance until we acquire possession of it, to the praise of his glory.

In the heavenly places

This section of Ephesians 1 is one long, flowing thought; a single sentence in the original Greek. The English Standard Version of the Bible aptly titles this section, "Spiritual Blessings in Christ." Before we unpack the depth of our spiritual blessings in Christ, I want to begin our look at this section with the last phrase from verse 3, "in the heavenly places." This phrase is pretty important to Ephesians, and Paul repeats it several times in the book. In chapter 1, verse 20, Christ is seated in the heavenly places. In chapter 2, verse 6, God has raised us up and seated us with him in the heavenly places. In chapter 3, verse 10, the church is a testimony in the heavenly places to the wisdom of God. And in chapter 6, verse 12, we wrestle against spiritual forces in heavenly places.

Here is the first thing we must grasp to get the whole of Paul's message to the church at Ephesus. There is more going on in your life than meets the eye! We have two realities at work—that which is seen and that which is unseen. The things that are happening out of our line of vision are just as real and relevant to our daily lives as anything we experience visually. Something big is going on in the heavenly places. Understanding our heavenly reality and all that is going on behind the scenes for us spiritually is of fundamental importance to get anything else Paul talks about in this book. Stott points this out in his commentary.

At this point it may be wise to pause a moment and consider how much all of us need to develop Paul's broad perspective. Let me remind you that he was a prisoner in Rome. Not indeed in a cell or dungeon, but still under house arrest and handcuffed to a Roman soldier. Yet, though his wrist was chained and his body was confined, his heart and mind inhabited eternity. … As for us, how blinkered is our vision in comparison with his, how small is our mind, how narrow are our horizons! Easily and naturally we clip into a preoccupation with our own petty little affairs. But we need to see time in the light of eternity, and our present privileges and obligations in the light of our past election and future perfection.[5]

We are talking about godly perspective—our outlook; our point of view; how we judge the relative significance of related events. From what angle do you view the variety of situations you face during a given day? Consider these verses on the perspective we get from a right focus on our heavenly reality:

> 2 Corinthians 4:17-18 For this light momentary affliction is preparing for us an eternal weight of glory beyond all comparison, as we look not to the things that are seen but to the things that are unseen. For the things that are seen are transient, but the things that are unseen are eternal.

> Colossians 3:1-3 If then you have been raised with Christ, seek the things that are above, where Christ is, seated at the right hand of God. Set your minds on things that are above, not on things that are on earth. For you have died, and your life is hidden with Christ in God.

Unlike the exhortation in these verses, my tendency is to look to my earthly reality to define me. My natural response is to see my daily circumstances as the absolute truth and interpret my view of eternity based on what I experience in life. I lack godly perspective. I am looking at my life from the wrong point of view. Paul here calls on us to do the exact opposite. It is our heavenly reality that has eternal value. Our earthly reality is transient, temporary, and fleeting. It simply does not endure. We must use our eternal, enduring reality in heaven as the unchanging focal point from which we determine meaning for our passing earthly reality.

Reflections

_____
_____
_____
_____
_____
_____
_____
_____

---

[5] Stott, p. 44-45.

Chapter 3 Ephesians 1: 3-14 continued

The end of the last chapter leads naturally to the question, "What exactly is my heavenly reality?" This brings us back to the title the ESV gives this section of Scripture—our "Spiritual Blessings in Christ." Read again verse 3, "Blessed be the God and Father of our Lord Jesus Christ, who has blessed us in Christ with every spiritual blessing in the heavenly places." We will examine two phrases here—"in Christ" and "every spiritual blessing."

In Christ

Here is the key to unpacking everything Paul is teaching in Ephesians. The phrases "in Christ", "in him", "before him," and "through him" dominate this book. In Chapter 1 alone, we are saturated with examples.

v. 4 "he chose us in him" to be "blameless before him"
v. 7 "in him we have redemption through his blood"
v. 9 "according to his purpose, which he set forth in Christ"
v. 10 "to unite all things in him"
v. 11 "In him we have obtained an inheritance"
v. 12 "we who were the first to hope in Christ"
v. 13 "in him" you were sealed in the Spirit, "in him" you believed

All our past, present, and future spiritual benefits—pretty much everything we talk about from this point on in Ephesians—flows from, in, and through Christ. This reminds me of Christ's words of himself in John 15:5, "I am the vine; you are the branches. Whoever abides in me and I in him, he it is that bears much fruit, for apart from me you can do nothing."

This is our spiritual reality. As believers, we are IN CHRIST. Yet, the fact that this is our reality does not necessarily mean we live in the full benefits this reality provides. II Peter 1 gives interesting insight into this tension. In verse 4, Peter says that God has "granted to us his precious and very great promises" so that we may "become partakers of the divine nature" of Christ. Then in verse 8, he gives sober instructions to guard us from "being ineffective or unfruitful in the knowledge of our Lord Jesus Christ."

Shortly, we are going to explore the "very great promises" we have in Christ. But for a moment, consider Peter's warning. Before we unpack the wealth of God's promises in Christ, we should make sure we understand the battle to bring our thoughts into submission to the truth so that the things we learn of Jesus may bear fruit in our lives. In II Corinthians 10:5, Paul teaches us that we must "destroy arguments and every lofty opinion raised against the knowledge of God and take every thought captive to obey Christ." The terms "destroy" and "take captive" are terms of war. The idea is that there is a battle for our minds. We must destroy (refute and tear down) arguments that contradict or diminish what we know to be true about God. Then we must take our thoughts captive and make them submit to the truth. The same word for taking our thoughts captive is used in 2 Timothy 3:6, "For among them are those who creep into households and capture weak women, burdened with sins and led astray by various passions." To be honest, this is not my favorite verse in the Bible. On a bad day (when I am not taking my thoughts captive), it just seems sexist. But on a day when I am thinking honestly about my own nature, it reminds me that either I take my own thoughts captive and make them submit to the truth of God's Word, or I am a prime target for someone else coming in my life to take my thoughts captive, leading me away from Christ and into sin. Apparently, my thoughts left to themselves are not going to just naturally stay on spiritually healthy mental paths.

There is a battle for our minds. If you are like me, you are likely to focus first on what you **do**. But Scripture is clear that our minds are the first battlefield, well before our actions. What we **think** will determine all the rest. I cannot emphasize this enough throughout our study of Ephesians.

Isaiah 26:3 You keep him in perfect peace whose mind is stayed on you, because he trusts in you.

As we go forward in this study, are you prepared to do battle for your mind? I hope we will all determine right now to examine our thoughts and make them submit to the truth of Ephesians throughout this study.

Reflections

_____
_____
_____
_____
_____
_____
_____
_____
_____
_____
_____
_____
_____
_____
_____

Chapter 4 Ephesians 1:3-14 continued

Every spiritual blessing

Growing up in the church, I heard the term *blessing* most of my life. But while I used the term easily and often, even signing my emails "Blessings" at times, I never thought deeply about the meaning of the term. Consider this word for a minute. If I have the blessing of my college professor on a project, this means basically that I have his approval. Or if I say I enjoy the blessings of freedom, then I am saying that I enjoy the concrete benefits that freedom gives me. Similarly, when we hear the term blessing in Scripture, we can associate it with the ideas of approval, favor, and the resulting concrete benefits of having that approval.

Now that I am in Christ, I am endowed with every spiritual blessing. Every last one! There is no spiritual blessing available to which I do not have access in Christ, and these blessings represent **concrete benefits that give testimony to God's favor on me**. Wow! Personally, I like to stop right here, park for a little while, and ponder the fact that I have been blessed by God in such an all-encompassing way—that God withholds no spiritual benefit from me and that his favor is on me in all ways spiritually. My problem is that I tend to maximize my focus on the word *blessing* and minimize my focus on the word *spiritual*. My idea of blessings tends to be whatever circumstantial change will ease my burdens or fears of the moment. But Paul specifically says *spiritual* blessings—concrete benefits that transcend our circumstances and transform us in deeper, richer, fuller ways. Make no mistake—these blessings definitely affect us in our earthly circumstances, but they are deep, eternal things working for us in the heavenly places. They are spiritual.

Thankfully, we are not left to speculate about what exactly Paul means when he uses the phrase, *every spiritual blessing*. The rest of this passage tells us exactly what blessings Paul is talking about.

4 even as he chose us in him before the foundation of the world, that we should be holy and blameless before him. In love 5 he predestined us for adoption as sons through Jesus Christ, according to the purpose of his will, 6 to the praise of his glorious grace, with which he has blessed us in the Beloved. 7 In him we have redemption through his blood, the forgiveness of our trespasses, according to the riches of his grace, 8 which he lavished upon us, in all wisdom and insight 9 making known to us the mystery of his will, according to his purpose, which he set forth in Christ 10 as a plan for the fullness of time, to unite all things in him, things in heaven and things on earth.

11 In him we have obtained an inheritance, having been predestined according to the purpose of him who works all things according to the counsel of his will, 12 so that we who were the first to hope in Christ might be to the praise of his glory. 13 In him you also, when you heard the word of truth, the gospel of your salvation, and believed in him, were sealed with the promised Holy Spirit, 14 who is the guarantee of our inheritance until we acquire possession of it, to the praise of his glory.

I have wrestled over how much time I should take to explore each of these individual spiritual blessings. If I write briefly on these blessings, do I convey that they are not worthy of long study? Many great theologians have written long, deep works on each of the spiritual acts outlined here—election, predestination, redemption, and adoption. I have resigned myself to the fact that I can never completely plumb the depths of this passage—that the spiritual concepts Paul discusses here are deeper and wider than I have the ability to fully understand myself, let alone describe to others. Instead, my hope is that the discussion we have here will be a starting point for a lifetime of your own future study and meditation.

So what are the spiritual blessings we have in Christ?

v. 4	He chose us in Christ before the foundation of the world.
v. 5	He predestined us for adoption as sons.
v. 6	He has blessed us with his glorious grace; v. 8 lavishing it upon us.
v. 7	He has redeemed us through his blood and forgiven our trespasses.
v. 9	He has made known to us the mystery of his will.
v. 11	We have obtained an inheritance.
v. 13	This inheritance is sealed and guaranteed by the Holy Spirit.

In a nutshell, Paul gives us the heart of our hope in Christ. He has it summed up succinctly and there is much here to unpack.

Chosen before time began to be holy and blameless before him

Paul does not use complicated language here, and I doubt I need to spend time defining any of these individual terms. The fact that the language is simple only amplifies the depth of the actual concept he presents. My husband and I have often talked about our burning need to be a part of something bigger than our mundane existence. I have two small boys, and one could well argue that raising them is the most important job I will ever have. Yet, I am worn out with the tedious nature of it all—feeding, bathing, diapering, potty training, disciplining, supporting, and answering an infinite number of unanswerable questions. These things fill my day and mentally wear me out, and the idea that perseverance for the next eighteen years will hopefully result in respectable young men who contribute to society is not enough to sustain me right now. I need an even greater purpose to keep me joyfully steadfast for the long haul.

In this passage, Paul gives us a deep spiritual truth—he calls us to understand God's purposes and plans from before creation. As fleeting as this life is, we can all marvel at something timeless and eternal. Our place in God's story was planned before time began. He chose us! He chose us for himself to accomplish his purposes and to reveal to the entire world something beautiful about himself. When I think of God setting his purposes in motion before time began and those purposes including me, then I start to tap into something that sustains me. I am not raising my boys simply to be responsible citizens when they turn eighteen and leave my house. I am raising them in light of God's eternal kingdom purposes for both them and me. The tedious aspects of my daily life fade as I get a vision for God's eternal plan playing out in my home. There is something going on here that transcends time and therefore gives meaning to this day, this week, this month, this year, and this lifetime.

In particular, God chose us to be holy (set apart) and blameless (faultless, morally free of guilt). The words *to be* indicate that this was not our state when he did the initial choosing. I was neither holy nor blameless when God chose me for himself. But his plan before time began was to make me (and my boys) into something we could never accomplish on our own—his own children set apart for his purposes and morally free from guilt.

Here we begin the difficult discussion on election—God's definitive choosing of us for salvation by his own will and not any work of our own. Some argue that the doctrine of election reduces Christians to robots with no personality or choice of their own. In contrast, the illustration the Bible uses is not that we were robots, but that we were slaves to sin, unable to free ourselves (Romans 6). Slaves have feelings, desires, hopes, and dreams. What they do not have is free choice. We were slaves to a master from which we could not free ourselves. But God chose before time began to set us free and change us completely. I appreciate Paul's words on this in Romans 8.

> 29 For those whom he foreknew he also predestined to be conformed to the image of his Son, in order that he might be the firstborn among many brothers. 30 And those whom he predestined he also called, and those whom he called he also justified, and those whom he justified he also glorified.

> 31 What then shall we say to these things? If God is for us, who can be against us? 32 He who did not spare his own Son but gave him up for us all, how will he not also with him graciously give us all things? 33 Who shall bring any charge against God's elect? It is God who justifies. 34 Who is to condemn? Christ Jesus is the one who died—more than that, who was raised—who is at the right hand of God, who indeed is interceding for us.

As Paul points out here, the result of a right understanding of this doctrine should be great confidence. If God is for me, who can be against me?! There is no accusation Satan can bring against me that will stick because Jesus died for me and now stands at God's side in heaven as my advocate. In giving his own son for me, he has proven himself gracious to me, withholding no blessing from me that I need. When we interpret God's choosing of us as the Bible presents it, it is a good, gracious, freeing gift from God.

Predestined for adoption as his sons

The Greek word translated predestined in verse 5 means to determine, appoint, or decide beforehand.[6] As I said earlier, context is everything in Ephesians. To really understand this phrase, we need to read it with the verses immediately before and after it as well.

> 4 even as he chose us in him before the foundation of the world, that we should be holy and blameless before him. In love 5 he predestined us for adoption as sons through Jesus Christ, according to the purpose of his will, 6 to the praise of his glorious grace, with which he has blessed us in the Beloved.

---

[6] Strongs, s. v. "proorizo."

I do not understand why the verse notations here break off the phrase "in love" from the beginning of verse 5. These verse divisions were not added until the mid 16ᵗʰ century. Legend has it that the translator made the divisions while on horseback traveling through France, which may explain the odd placement in this particular sentence.

The phrase "in love" is fundamental to understanding what Paul is communicating in verse 5. Our tendency is to focus on the term predestined. Self-determination is highly valued in western cultures. I live in the Pacific Northwest. We were settled by a crazy bunch of independent minded people in the mid 1800's. They and their progeny have made sure this area of the country values independence and self-determination to a degree I have never seen before. I like it here, because I am as hardheaded and independent thinking as the next guy. The idea of my destiny being determined for me before time began is a hard pill to swallow.

Ephesians 1 reveals the hard truth that self-determination is a myth. While I hate that idea at times, deep down in the depth of my heart, I know it is true. Even more than that, ultimately it is comforting, for my efforts to determine my own destiny have failed and frustrated me time and time again. When I get past the term predestined, I can focus on the important qualifying phrases that describe God's motivation and intent in determining my destiny before time began. His motivation is love, and his intent is that I be adopted into his family with all the full benefits and privileges available to children of the Most High. The concept of adoption is itself worthy of its own separate book. I recommend *Adopted for Life* by Russell Moore for an in-depth look at the theological and practical parallels between earthly adoption and our adoption by God into his family.

God determined my destiny before time began because he loves me and he wants to pour his blessings on me as his child. Does that grip your heart? Does that move you to tears? We need to meditate on this phrase until the truths steep deeply into our minds. This is a spiritual blessing that, when properly understood, has the power to sustain us in deep trials.

Reflections

_____

_____

_____

_____

_____

_____

_____

_____

_____

_____

_____

Chapter 5 Ephesians 1:6-14

He has blessed us with his glorious grace; lavishing it upon us

By nature, I am a stingy cheap wad. When it comes time to leave a tip at a restaurant, I calculate the percentage to the penny, considering myself generous if I round up a penny at the end. In contrast, my husband shames me with his generosity to others. I appreciate his generosity to me, but I am not nearly as gracious when he extends it to others. In short, generosity is not my strong suit. When Paul says that God has *lavished* his grace upon us, I am struck by the wording. God has not rationed out his grace on us. Unlike me, he does not calculate exactly and round to the nearest cent. He abundantly exceeds our needs. He pours his grace out on us so that it overflows. He furnishes us in rich measure.

Furthermore, his grace poured out on us in abundant measure is *glorious*. The Greek word here indicates magnificence, excellence, and splendor.[7] He has lavished us with an excellent grace, a magnificent loving-kindness. His favor and approval on us is splendid.

Gifts are my love language. I remember one birthday in particular when my husband surprised me with two tickets to *The Lord of the Rings*, which was showing the night of my birthday for the last time at the Cinerama, a local large screen theater that made you feel like you were right there riding a horse into battle against Sauron. I wanted to go so badly, but my husband worked evenings. The really neat thing about the gift was that he surprised me by taking the day off of work to go with me. He had gone out of his way to be thoughtful. His gift far exceeded my expectations, and I felt well loved from that gift for some time.

When I hear that God has lavished his loving-kindness on me and then meditate on all that means, it makes a difference in how I think about my daily life. He has exceeded my expectations, lavishing me with a glorious gift, and I feel his love on me when I meditate on this phrase of Scripture. God has spoken to me in my love language.

He has redeemed us through his blood and forgiven our trespasses

I like the word *redeemed*. Here, it is directly related to the forgiveness of sins. Consider also Colossians 1:13-14.

> He has delivered us from the domain of darkness and transferred us to the kingdom of his beloved Son, in whom we have redemption, the forgiveness of sins.

The Greek word translated *redeemed* in both Ephesians and Colossians means to release or liberate by paying a ransom.[8] The implication is that someone or something held us hostage. We have

---

[7] Strongs, s. v. "doxa."

talked briefly about our slavery to sin. Now it is time to understand more of what Scripture teaches on spiritual slavery. We cannot understand our redemption if we do not understand our slavery.

In Romans 6, the Apostle Paul refers multiple times to our slavery to sin and our freedom from its dominion in Christ.

v. 6 We know that our old self was crucified with him in order that the body of sin might be brought to nothing, so that we would no longer be enslaved to sin.

v. 14 For sin will have no dominion over you, since you are not under law but under grace.

v. 17 But thanks be to God, that you who were once slaves of sin have become obedient from the heart to the standard of teaching to which you were committed.

v. 18 and having been set free from sin, have become slaves of righteousness.

v. 22 But now that you have been set free from sin and have become slaves of God, the fruit you get leads to sanctification and its end, eternal life.

In Romans 8, Paul further clarifies the contrast between our slavery to sin before Christ and our new freedom and status in God's family in Christ.

v. 1-2 There is therefore now no condemnation for those who are in Christ Jesus. For the law of the Spirit of life has set you free in Christ Jesus from the law of sin and death.

v. 14-15 For all who are led by the Spirit of God are sons of God. For you did not receive the spirit of slavery to fall back into fear, but you have received the Spirit of adoption as sons, by whom we cry, "Abba! Father!"

While we were slaves to sin, Christ died for us and set us free from sin's rule over us. He did not pay our penalty for sin just for us to consider ourselves slaves in his household, though in my estimation, that would be reasonable. Instead, God gives us two different human pictures to define the honored position in which he has set us in his household. First, in Romans 8 and Ephesians 1, we see that we are God's adopted children, loved and treasured as a "fellow heir with Christ" (Romans 8:17). Then, in Ephesians 5, Paul speaks of us as the beloved bride of Christ. I would like to look at the second picture for a moment.

The book of Hosea in the Old Testament gives us a beautiful picture of God's pursuit of his wayward bride and is one of the clearest presentations of our slavery to sin and subsequent redemption by God. The prophet Hosea preaches a message of repentance to God's people against the backdrop of his own personal story, written and directed by God. By order of God, Hosea marries the harlot Gomer. They have a child together, but Gomer then has children through adultery with other men. Hosea receives her back, along with her other children. Gomer returns yet again to the life of a harlot and eventually becomes a slave, unable to return to Hosea

---

[8] Strongs, s. v. "apulotrosis."

even if she had wanted. All under the direction of God, Hosea buys her back at public auction. However, he does not buy her to use her as a slave. Instead, Hosea restores her to the honored position of his wife and helper, the lady of his household. God draws a direct correlation between Hosea's redemption of Gomer out of slavery and God's redemption of his own people.

Hosea 2:15-16 (NIV)
15 There I will give her back her vineyards,
    and will make the Valley of Achor a door of hope.
    There she will sing as in the days of her youth,
    as in the day she came up out of Egypt.
16 "In that day," declares the LORD,
    "you will call me 'my husband';
    you will no longer call me 'my master.'"

God pays our ransom, releasing us from the payment we owe for sin by paying for it himself in the form of Christ's death on the cross. The direct result is the forgiveness of our sins. The debt for our sin is cancelled. We owe no more payment, and now, in Christ, no one can condemn us (Romans 8:1). We are free!

I am a mix of pride and shame—pride when I get it right, shame when I mess things up. Understanding redemption frees me from both. I cannot hold on to my pride—for I know I was a slave to sin and it is only through God's grace I have been freed. Yet, I cannot dwell in shame either—for God willingly and purposefully sought me out to pay for my sins and to establish me in his household in a high and honored position. Meditating on the grace seen in his redemption eases my struggle between pride and shame, bringing me great peace.

He has made known to us the mystery of his will

I especially like how the New American Standard Version translates Ephesians 1:8-9.

… In all wisdom and insight He made known to us the mystery of His will, according to His kind intention which He purposed in Him.

God is letting us know something deep and wonderful about his purposes and plans, and his motivation for revealing himself to us is his *kind intention*. The Greek word here indicates good will, benevolence, delight, pleasure, or satisfaction.[9] God delights in us, and it is his pleasure in us that causes him to tell us these deep things about himself.

I am choosy about the people to whom I open myself, mostly out of self-protection. It is scary to let myself be known by those who might abuse their knowledge, so I protect the deeper things about myself, sharing my innermost hopes and plans with only a select few. However, despite my guardedness on opening up myself, I still have a lot to learn about being a good steward of someone else's confidence when they reveal themselves to me. Often, I am simply oblivious. I miss that this person just revealed a piece of himself or herself to me, and I go on with my own

---

[9] Strongs, s. v. "eudokia."

self-centered side of the conversation. I have a good friend who has taught me much about my failures this way simply through her consistent example. When I open myself to her, she stops. She listens. She thinks. Then she responds, and her response is usually a follow up question that pursues an even deeper understanding of me.

How do you react when Paul says that God has revealed himself to you? Do you see it as a precious privilege? Do you want to be a good steward of this treasure? Do you desire to know more? Or do you gloss over it, running ahead to the next thing on your mind? If we are really listening and engaged in this conversation, then our next question should be, "God, what exactly is this mystery that you are revealing to me?" Ephesians 1:10 gives the answer. God is revealing his "plan for the fullness of time, to unite all things in him, things in heaven and things on earth." Colossians 1:16-20 also speaks to this.

16 For by him *(Christ)* all things were created, in heaven and on earth, visible and invisible, whether thrones or dominions or rulers or authorities—all things were created through him and for him. 17 And he is before all things, and in him all things hold together. 18 And he is the head of the body, the church. He is the beginning, the firstborn from the dead, that in everything he might be preeminent. 19 For in him all the fullness of God was pleased to dwell, 20 and through him to reconcile to himself all things, whether on earth or in heaven, making peace by the blood of his cross.

Does this sound a bit mysterious to you? What does it mean to be reconciled to Christ and united with him? Paul refers to this uniting of Christ and creation as a mystery, and in the coming chapters of Ephesians, he will explain much more about this mystery—namely, the supernatural relationship between Christ and the church. This is the mystery of God's will that he is graciously revealing to us. But what does this mean exactly? Some people might read Paul's words and say, "That's simple." They will read this Scripture quickly and dismiss it as something they already basically understand. These people likely will not take time to think through the concepts here, because they are, to be brutally honest, too proud or self-centered to recognize their ignorance on this subject. Others of us recognize that this is indeed a mystery, and there is a depth of meaning here with which we must engage our hearts and minds to understand. In this second category, we have two choices. We can say, "This is too hard to understand. I'll just leave it to pastors and seminary students to deal with this." Or we can say, "God is revealing something deep about himself to me, and I want to understand it."

When I am not chasing my children or writing books during their naptime, my other job is community college math instructor. When getting my degrees in math education, I had times when I faced difficult subject matter. Sometimes the difficult concepts seemed so completely irrelevant to anything I might ever do in life that I only applied myself to understand just enough to pass the class. But on occasion, I faced challenging material that I knew was also quite relevant to life. It was no easier to navigate, but the fact that I knew it mattered made me persist at understanding it. The mystery of God's purposes that he is revealing to us now in Ephesians MATTERS. It may not be simple to understand, but it is worth staying engaged until you do.

The rest of Ephesians gives us both contrasting and complementary pictures of this mystery. As we look at each section in the next chapters individually, we must put them all together in context to see the full picture of the great plan God is revealing to us here.

We have already read in verse 5 that God determined before time began to adopt us into his family. This adoption comes with every last benefit available to a child by birth. We are not the ugly stepsisters in the house of God. This is reflected clearly in how Scripture talks of our inheritance as God's children. Read again from Romans 8.

> For you did not receive a spirit that makes you a slave again to fear, but you received the Spirit of sonship. And by him we cry, "Abba, Father." The Spirit himself testifies with our spirit that we are God's children. Now if we are children, then we are heirs—heirs of God and *co-heirs* with Christ, if indeed we share in his sufferings in order that we may also share in his glory....The creation waits in eager expectation for the sons of God to be revealed....Not only so, but we ourselves, who have the firstfruits of the Spirit, groan inwardly as we wait eagerly for our adoption as sons, the redemption of our bodies. For in this hope we were saved.[10]

When I read this passage, I am struck by the phrase "*co-heir* with Christ." When I first heard this phrase, I reacted with disbelief. It seemed to border on heresy to think of myself as an heir of God on par with God the Son. Regardless, this is exactly how God wants me to think of my position in his family. We are not adopted into God's family as a token charity case. We are adopted into his family with the highest of honors and the greatest of inheritances.

In Galatians, Paul again talks about our honored position and inheritance as God's children.

> You are all sons of God through faith in Christ Jesus, for all of you who were baptized into Christ have clothed yourselves with Christ...But when the time had fully come, God sent his Son, born of a woman, born under law, to redeem those under law, that *we might receive the full rights of sons*. Because you are sons, God sent the Spirit of his Son into our hearts, the Spirit who calls out, "Abba, Father." So you are no longer a slave, but a son; and since you are a son, God has made you also an heir.[11]

Again, we see that we are not second rate citizens in God's household but his own dear children with full rights of inheritance.

The great truth of the inheritance I have as a child of God and co-heir with Christ is that it is **secure**. I do not have to worry that I will lose this inheritance because the Holy Spirit is the deposit and guarantee that God will fulfill his commitment to me.

> Now it is God who makes both us and you stand firm in Christ. He anointed us, set his seal of ownership on us, and put his Spirit in our hearts as a deposit, guaranteeing what is to come.[12]

God the Spirit is described as the deposit, guarantee, and seal of our salvation. Consider the meanings of these terms. A deposit is something given as assurance that an obligation will be met. When we guarantee something, we are making a pledge that a particular outcome will be

---

[10] Romans 8:15-17, 19, 23 NIV.
[11] Galatians 3:26-27; 4:4-7, NIV, emphasis mine.
[12] 2 Corinthians 1:21-22, NIV.

accomplished in a specified manner. If we set our seal on something, that seal serves as assurance that binds us to complete it. To summarize, deposits, guarantees, and seals hold people to their word. This is what God has done for us through the Holy Spirit. He has given us something that assures us with absolute certainty that he is going to keep his word.

I have had many people break their word to me over the years and disappoint me with their lack of follow through on commitments they have made to me. I am deeply moved by the depths to which God has gone in this great plan of his to assure me that he will not default on his promises to me. He has given himself to me in the form of the Holy Spirit. He does not leave me as an orphan to navigate this world on my own. Instead, he lives in me himself as the direct link between my earthly reality and my spiritual inheritance in Christ.

We have discussed the individual spiritual blessings Paul lists in this section of Ephesians. However, taking them apart individually does not allow us to fully appreciate the interrelatedness of each. So, with our collection of thoughts on each specific phrase in mind, read verses 4 through 14 once again in context, noting the ebb and flow of one blessing into the next.

> 4 even as he chose us in him before the foundation of the world, that we should be holy and blameless before him. In love 5 he predestined us for adoption as sons through Jesus Christ, according to the purpose of his will, 6 to the praise of his glorious grace, with which he has blessed us in the Beloved. 7 In him we have redemption through his blood, the forgiveness of our trespasses, according to the riches of his grace, 8 which he lavished upon us, in all wisdom and insight 9 making known to us the mystery of his will, according to his purpose, which he set forth in Christ 10 as a plan for the fullness of time, to unite all things in him, things in heaven and things on earth.

> 11 In him we have obtained an inheritance, having been predestined according to the purpose of him who works all things according to the counsel of his will, 12 so that we who were the first to hope in Christ might be to the praise of his glory. 13 In him you also, when you heard the word of truth, the gospel of your salvation, and believed in him, were sealed with the promised Holy Spirit, 14 who is the guarantee of our inheritance until we acquire possession of it, to the praise of his glory.

In Christ, we are indeed blessed with every spiritual blessing. Now, we must begin to understand how this spiritual reality equips us in our earthly reality.

Reflections

_____

_____

_____

_____

_____

_____

_____

_____

Chapter 6 Ephesians 1:15-23

15 For this reason, because I have heard of your faith in the Lord Jesus and your love toward all the saints, 16 I do not cease to give thanks for you, remembering you in my prayers, 17 that the God of our Lord Jesus Christ, the Father of glory, may give you a spirit of wisdom and of revelation in the knowledge of him, 18 having the eyes of your hearts enlightened, that you may know what is the hope to which he has called you, what are the riches of his glorious inheritance in the saints, 19 and what is the immeasurable greatness of his power toward us who believe, according to the working of his great might 20 that he worked in Christ when he raised him from the dead and seated him at his right hand in the heavenly places, 21 far above all rule and authority and power and dominion, and above every name that is named, not only in this age but also in the one to come. 22 And he put all things under his feet and gave him as head over all things to the church, 23 which is his body, the fullness of him who fills all in all.

This section is a prayer of thanksgiving to God for our inheritance in Christ and a petition for a deeper understanding of all we have in him. Paul prays for a *spirit of wisdom and of revelation in the knowledge of him*. The call to wisdom will be repeated by Paul throughout Ephesians. The best definition I have heard of wisdom as Paul uses it in Ephesians is *skill in the art of gospel living*. Keep that definition in mind as we progress through this study.

Paul in his request for greater knowledge, revelation, and wisdom prays that we would *know* three key things: the *hope* of our calling, the *riches* of Christ's inheritance, and the *power* at work on our behalf. However, before we move deeply into this prayer, note the first words of this section of Scripture.

For this reason

If you need any more evidence that the book of Ephesians is one long, flowing, connected thought, here it is. Paul writes a beautiful prayer of thanksgiving in this section of Scripture, but it loses its meaning completely if we do not directly tie it to the reasons for it—our heavenly reality in Christ which Paul described in verses 3-14.

Because God determined before time began to adopt us into his family, to redeem us from our sins, to lavish his grace on us, to reveal his plans to us, and to give us his Spirit as a seal on us to guarantee our inheritance as his children, we enter this prayer of thanksgiving. Paul is in essence saying, "Because God has poured out his blessings on us in all of these ways, wake up and take notice!" Verses 15-23 show us clearly the value of our spiritual inheritance by way of Paul's response in thanksgiving for it all.

That you may know

We referred earlier to Peter's warning in 2 Peter 1 against an ineffective understanding of the precious promises we have in Christ. There, Peter warns of a nearsighted view of life because we have forgotten the heart of the gospel, the forgiveness of our sins (2 Pet. 1:9). Paul's prayer here in Ephesians 1 echoes the same ideas. Paul cries out to God that we would possess a spirit of wisdom and revelation in the knowledge of him. This reminds me how utterly dependent I am on God to reveal himself to me. The psalmist prays in Psalms 119:18, "Open my eyes, that I may behold wondrous things out of your law." He recognizes his dependence on God to open his eyes to the beautiful truths of Scripture. This must be our prayer at this point of our study as well. "God, we want to know you and understand what you are showing us here. Open our eyes that we may understand fully all you are revealing to us about yourself."

John Stott notes that some Christians "lay such emphasis on the undoubted truth that everything is already theirs in Christ, that they become complacent and appear to have no appetite to know or experience their Christian privileges more deeply. … What Paul does in Ephesians 1, and therefore encourages us to copy, is both to keep praising God that in Christ all spiritual blessings are ours and to keep praying that we may know the fullness of what he has given us."[13] I have known Christians who fit Stott's description. Because they can quote their church's doctrinal statement complete with Scripture references, they think they fully understand their blessings in Christ and no longer need to wrestle with God to know him and his promises more deeply. That is foolishness indeed. Paul calls on us here to prayerfully stay engaged with God over the gospel for the rest of our lives—looking to him daily to understand our hope and power for living.

The hope of your calling

In verses 3-14, Paul dealt with the facts of our calling. Now he calls on us to attach to it an emotion—hope. Paul's prayer is that you and I may know "the hope to which he has called you." As I type this, I realize that while I understand the facts of my calling, it is another thing entirely to understand the hope that should come with it. Hope as used in this verse indicates a joyful expectation. There is something about my spiritual inheritance in Christ that should produce an expectation that sustains me long term. My problem is that I am a woman of weak endurance. When my expectations are not quickly fulfilled, my patience fades along with my hope, and I sit staring off in my rocking chair morosely wondering why things are not now the way I expected them to be. The entire point of hope is that it is joyful expectation of future fulfillment. It would not be hope if we had it all in our sight right now. Hope is the key to endurance. None of us can run the Christian marathon without hope in all God has revealed to us about the coming finish line. Paul knows our frailties well and therefore prays earnestly for our hope—supernatural, joyful expectation that endures for the long haul. I am learning to make this a part of my own prayers as well. "God, give me an expectation of the coming fulfillment of your eternal promises that lasts for the long haul and equips me to joyfully endure through the dry seasons of life."

---

[13] Stott, p. 52.

The riches of his inheritance

This phrase reminds me of one of the illustrations I used to open this book—the story of Hetty Green who inherited millions and yet lived like a pauper. She is one of many famous misers. They are known for having access to great wealth, but instead of using it to benefit themselves and their families, they live in substandard conditions. Instead of knowing the wealth of their inheritance, they fear that they will loose their riches and therefore hoard it irrationally. They do not see their wealth as something that has enough long-term value that they can use it in this very moment. The term miser is closely related to the term miserable, and both have their root in the Latin word for unhappy or wretched.[14] Paul's prayer here is that we who are tempted to live as spiritual misers would instead walk daily with an appropriate understanding of the wealth at our fingertips as children of God. You can recognize a spiritual miser because they are wretched and unhappy despite their inheritance in Christ. They believe in Christ, but they are still miserable. Are you there? I have been a miserable Christian at many points in my life. The key to change is so simple. Avail yourself of your spiritual wealth! For me, this means turning to God in prayer. "God, I want to understand my spiritual wealth in you. Teach me what it looks like to apply the riches of my inheritance to this situation I am in right now. Keep me from responding like an unhappy spiritual miser."

Note that Paul specifically prays that we may know *what are the riches of HIS glorious inheritance in the saints*. He is speaking now of this inheritance from a different angle. We are Jesus' riches. In Ephesians 5, we will talk more about this when we read of Christ's love for his church and his giving of himself for her. This whole concept gives me great pause. God has given me great things in Christ. I understand that. But I am the great thing that God has given Christ? I am HIS rich inheritance?! Oh, this humbles me and honors me at the same time. I know I am unworthy to be valued so highly by God. But it transforms me deeply to know that Christ treasures me this way.

The power at work on your behalf

There are many phrases in Ephesians that have deeply moved me, especially here at the end of chapter one. But this one has caused me to stop and meditate again and again. Paul prays that we would know (perceive, pay attention to, discern) the power at work for us who are in Christ.[15] Then he goes on to describe the greatness of this power, "the working of his great might that he worked in Christ when he raised him from the dead and seated him at his right hand in the heavenly places." Wow! The power at work on my behalf is the SAME POWER GOD USED TO RAISE CHRIST FROM THE DEAD! Stop here for a moment. Meditate on this. Many times I feel helpless, frustrated, and anemic. I cannot stop the tide of frustrations life throws my way, and I know better than anyone what I lack in endurance. When I stop, pray for understanding, and spend time meditating on this passage, my entire outlook changes. What hope

---

[14] miser. Dictionary.com. *Online Etymology Dictionary*. Douglas Harper, Historian. http://dictionary.reference.com/browse/miser (accessed: June 04, 2008).

[15] Strongs, s. v. "eido."

it brings me to know that God is working in and through me with the same power that raised Christ from his stinking tomb to beautiful, walking perfection. When I face the frustrations and disappointments of life, I have access to supernatural, resurrection strength to miraculously transform my dead, stinking thought processes. Do you believe that the very power that raised Christ from the dead is at work for you right now? My prayer to God for us all is that we really understand the resurrection power at work for us. May God open our eyes to his ability to transform our attitudes and responses in spiritual freedom just as he released Christ from the bonds of death.

Paul has finished his first prayer of Ephesians but not his first thought. As we move into Ephesians 2, we will continue to see his connected flow of thought.

Reflections

_____

_____

_____

_____

_____

_____

_____

_____

_____

_____

_____

_____

_____

_____

_____

_____

_____

_____

_____

_____

_____

_____

Chapter 7 Ephesians 2:1-10

1 And you were dead in the trespasses and sins 2 in which you once walked, following the course of this world, following the prince of the power of the air, the spirit that is now at work in the sons of disobedience— 3 among whom we all once lived in the passions of our flesh, carrying out the desires of the body and the mind, and were by nature children of wrath, like the rest of mankind. 4 But God, being rich in mercy, because of the great love with which he loved us, 5 even when we were dead in our trespasses, made us alive together with Christ—by grace you have been saved— 6 and raised us up with him and seated us with him in the heavenly places in Christ Jesus, 7 so that in the coming ages he might show the immeasurable riches of his grace in kindness toward us in Christ Jesus. 8 For by grace you have been saved through faith. And this is not your own doing; it is the gift of God, 9 not a result of works, so that no one may boast. 10 For we are his workmanship, created in Christ Jesus for good works, which God prepared beforehand, that we should walk in them.

You were dead in sin

The situation Paul outlines in 2:1-3 is quite dire. What he summarizes in three verses here, he expounds with more detail in the first three chapters of the book of Romans. We were not just generally frustrated by our sin or mired down in the muck of our sin. No, our situation was much worse. We were DEAD in our sin—no heartbeat, decaying flesh kind of dead. Dead people do not make choices. Dead people do not resuscitate themselves. Dead people cannot unwrap their shrouds or open their tombs. In other words, our situation was utterly hopeless.

Paul reiterates the hopelessness of our status in verses 1-3 by going on to say that we were "by nature children of wrath." The word *nature* is key here. It means that the origin of our condition is rooted in the core of our being. We are innately *children of wrath*. We did not learn it—we were born into it. It is inherent in our nature. This is a hard statement to hear and reconcile with the compassion and love of God. Yet, God's wrath against us is actually fully consistent with both his love and mercy. God's wrath is not like ours. It is not bad temper, spite, or malice. God's wrath is not animosity or revenge. In particular, God's wrath is not arbitrary. His wrath is never subject to his mood or whim. Instead it is definite and predictable, and his wrath is always against evil.[16] I like John Stott's definition of God's wrath, "God's personal, righteous, constant hostility to evil, his settled refusal to compromise with it, and his resolve instead to condemn it."[17] If you are like me, you value consistency against evil, and we all want protection from evil. It is God's love and mercy that he does not allow evil to go unpunished. Our problem with this passage is that we do not like it when we realize that the evil is within us—that we are by nature children deserving of God's consistent, just hand against evil. It is okay with me when God is judging others but not so good when he is judging me.

---

[16] Stott, p. 75-76.
[17] Ibid, p. 76.

This is a hard but necessary word from God. We are all fully deserving of God's wrath. We were dead in our sins, mastered by evil. It is not until we fully understand the gravity of the human condition that we recognize the problem with people's immature beliefs in superficial cures to the human condition. What fool would enter a hospital's morgue with a crash cart from the emergency room expecting any results? The people in the morgue are dead—IV's, breathing tubes, and defibrillators are irrelevant now. The same goes for us spiritually. We did not need spiritual therapy. Our situation was way too dire for that. We needed total transformation—we needed a new life.

After summarizing the wretchedness of our condition before God in verses 1-3, Paul writes, in my opinion, the two most beautiful words in all of Scripture.

But God

But God—another short phrase from Scripture filled with profound meaning and therefore worthy of serious meditation. I love how Stott words his thoughts on this phrase.

> These two monosyllables set against the desperate condition of fallen mankind the gracious initiative and sovereign action of God. We were the objects of his wrath, *but God, out of the great love with which he loved us* had mercy upon us. We were dead, and dead men do not rise, *but God* made us alive with Christ. We were slaves, in a situation of dishonor and powerlessness, *but God* has raised us with Christ and set us at his own right hand, in a position of honor and power. Thus God has taken action to reverse our condition in sin. It is essential to hold both parts of this contrast together, namely what we are by nature and what we are by grace, the human condition and the divine compassion, God's wrath and God's love.[18]

When we were dead in our trespasses and sins and by nature children deserving of God's wrath, God intervened. He did not leave us that way. He did something about it. Why? Because he is *rich in mercy* and loves us with a *great love*. He is abounding and overflowing with compassion for the oppressed. I love the definition of the Greek word translated *mercy* in verse 4—" kindness or good will towards the miserable and the afflicted, joined with a desire to help them."[19] That is beautiful.

The key to understanding mercy is understanding our condition when God intervened—dead in our sins and deserving of God's wrath by our very nature. We were indeed miserable. But God looked on us and desired to help us, and his help has altered us in every way. He brought us from spiritual death to life completely by his great work and not of anything we had to offer, because dead men do not have anything to offer the doctor with which to heal them.

According to Paul, the practical evidence that we really understand this teaching is humility— we understand that we *cannot boast* (v. 9). We should stop and examine ourselves here for a moment. Humility is one of the greatest Christian virtues and yet also the one most often missing in the people who should best understand it. When in my 20's I first learned the doctrines of grace

---

[18] Stott, p. 79-80.
[19] Strongs, s. v. "eleos."

in Ephesians 1 and 2, I was amazed and humbled by the mercy of my Father in heaven. Then I started meeting other Christians who hold to the so-called doctrines of grace and spent time disillusioned by the disconnect between their theology and their practice. My experience is that we who hold tightly to these doctrines tend to be some of the least gracious people in Christianity. Shame on us. No matter how well we can articulate the doctrines of grace, if it is not well accompanied by humility, we deny our understanding of these doctrines completely.

We Christians have at times had a worldwide reputation for pride and arrogance. I read Christian books, magazines, and blogs daily, and I see that the proud, self-righteous Christian is still alive and well, speaking authoritatively on things of which he/she does not know and pronouncing judgment against others in ways that spit on the love and mercy that God has modeled for us all. If we really understand the juxtaposition between what we were inherently in our nature and what God did for us solely by his own love and mercy, we know we have nothing on anyone. Any doctrinal or personal conflict we have with another must be dominated by the Biblical characteristics of love, mercy, and humility. To do any less is to trample upon the grace of God toward us.

Saved by grace through faith

I learned Ephesians 2:8-9 in Sunday school as a child. One might think that being "saved by grace through faith" would be a fairly straightforward idea. But despite memorizing it, I did not really appreciate it for many years. I was intent on figuring out how to win and keep God's (and others') approval. Unconditional, unearned favor was completely beyond my grasp. I doubt I am alone in my misunderstanding of this Scripture, and Paul gives several clarifying statements to make sure we get the obvious—that we did not save ourselves.

v. 8   this is not your own doing
v. 9   it is the gift of God
v. 9   not a result of works
v. 10   we are his workmanship

Do you grasp what Paul is saying? We did not contribute in any way to this work God has done for us. He has done it in spite of us, not in conjunction with us. We were not helpers or facilitators. In fact, you could argue that we just got in the way. But Christ's death on the cross removed all the obstacles (our sin being the first and greatest), and he singularly made the way for us to have faith in him.

Created for good works

Paul goes on to point out that it is not only our salvation that is all of God and none of us, but that the subsequent good works that follow coming to faith in Christ are also the result of God's work within us. The implication is that our attempts to boast in any good work after our salvation are as naïve as our attempts to boast in the act that brought us to salvation. As we end this section of Ephesians, Paul paints a vivid contrast between what man is by nature (a child of wrath) and what he becomes by grace (created in Christ Jesus for good works).[20] We have seen our desperate state apart from God and God's intervention to change us in ways we could never change ourselves. Now we see what God has created us and changed us **for**.

Note the entirety of verse 10. "For we are his workmanship, created in Christ Jesus for good works, which God prepared beforehand, that we should walk in them." The term *workmanship* fits exactly with the phrase *created in Christ Jesus*. We are the product of God's creation, God's intervention, and God's planning for the purpose of "good works." The Greek word here is *agathos*, meaning useful, good, pleasant, agreeable, joyful, happy, excellent, distinguished, upright, or honorable.[21]

The closing salutation of Hebrews 13 gives more insight into this truth.

> 20 Now may the God of peace who brought again from the dead our Lord Jesus, the great shepherd of the sheep, by the blood of the eternal covenant, 21 equip you with everything good that you may do his will, working in us that which is pleasing in his sight, through Jesus Christ, to whom be glory forever and ever. Amen.

We are not just utterly dependent on God for our salvation, but also for every good work that flows from it for the rest of our lives. The picture here is not of robots—mechanical automatons under the remote control of their creator. Rather, this reflects the picture Jesus gives us in John 15:5, "I am the vine and you are the branches. … Apart from me you can do nothing." We are not talking about cold mechanics. This is an organic union of living beings. We are God's creation, united with Christ, and living out his good plan through this union. Our attempts at righteousness apart from this union will leave us withering on the ground, without nourishment for ourselves or fruit to show for our efforts. Apart from him, we can do nothing.

We have reached the end of this first section of Ephesians. Paul has set up for us a grand theme, our spiritual blessings in Christ, that influences everything else we read from this point on. We know both what we were before God found us and what he has done for us in Christ. We know that God has been intentional with this plan since before time began, that he has not withheld any good gift from us, that he has lavished his grace on us, and that the same power that raised Christ from the dead is at work on our behalf. This is his gift, we cannot boast, and this plan does not end at the moment of our salvation. No—God has prepared us for excellent, distinguished works in his name. We are new creatures on a new path, and now everything is different.

In light of all this, what is different for you? What aspects of your life reflect these truths? Where do they break down? In my life, it seems that there are places where these truths saturate my existence, other places where they lightly rain down, and many parched places where these truths seem to have not yet touched. At church and in Christian ministry, I am intentional about meditating on doctrine and applying it to life, but in the places closer to home, those places where I let down my guard and do not care to be on my best behavior, there are many parched areas in need of the soaking rain of these gospel truths.

---

[20] Stott, p. 69.
[21] Strongs, s. v. "agathos."

How do I move from my old, gospel-less ways of thinking to patterns of thought that reflect the truths of Ephesians 1 and 2? The answer is twofold—prayerful dependence upon God and intentional wrangling of my own thoughts. Scripture is clear that we are dependent on God for all of this, both the content of our salvation and our ability to let it permeate and transform our thought processes. So my first exhortation is to pray to God to open your eyes to the hope of your calling and the riches of your inheritance. Then in conjunction with prayer, examine your thought processes, lasso in wayward thoughts, and make them submit to the truth of Scripture.

Recently, I battled depression and discouragement over some unloving statements made toward me. I got hurt, then angry, then determined to become more lovable so people would not speak to me that way, and finally frustrated that I could not make myself any more lovable when I thought I was okay in the first place. It was a losing mental battle. Then I was reminded of God's words toward me in Ephesians 1. He chose me for his family and has lavished his grace on me because he loved me, even when I was most unlovable. His love for me is unconditional. I thought of God's words to His people in Jeremiah 31:3, "I have loved you with an everlasting love; I have drawn you with loving-kindness." Those are beautiful words, but they had not yet penetrated my heart so that they changed how I felt about myself and how I responded to my circumstances in that particular moment. I had to wrangle my thoughts. I had to wrestle with God, "You have loved me with an everlasting love, Father. But I do not feel very loved or lovable right now. Please plug these truths into my heart that they would change me forever. **Help me respond now not as someone desperate for love, but someone secure in the love of her Father**." The process of understanding these truths has not been easy or quick, at least not for me. It has taken genuine effort on my part, clinging to God and struggling with my thought patterns. But at some point in the process, I started to get it. God loves me, and his love sustains me in a way that is deep and transforming. He has pursued me from before time began, and even in this moment when I feel unloved by others, his love for me is lavish. It is real. As I meditate on my spiritual blessings in Christ, I can tell the moment these truths stop being head knowledge and start seeping down into my heart.

Do not be content to simply read through these thoughts and then tuck them away like a miser. Your spiritual inheritance is useful right now in the issues you face daily in life. Spend your inheritance hour by hour of each day, raising your children, loving your husband, adjusting to coworkers, supporting your roommate, dealing with your family, dealing with your church. Your inheritance in Christ is of infinite value and relevant to what you are facing right now. You will never spend it all.

Reflections

_____

_____

_____

_____

_____

Section 2 Ephesians 2:11 – 3:21

While studying through the book of Ephesians at a women's retreat a few years ago, many of the women at the retreat verbalized that this next section of the book was the hardest for them to get. But this section also holds some of the richest treasures in the book. The content centers on the themes of alienation and reconciliation, and many of us can identify with these themes. The term *alienation* resonates with me. It means to be excluded and shut out from intimacy and fellowship.[22] I have spent my fair share of time feeling alienated and excluded from people and places where I longed for intimacy and fellowship, even within the Body of Christ. It is a lonely place.

In my experience, it is sin and false idols that alienate me from others and others from me. When the moment comes that the sin is addressed and forgiven, reconciliation occurs. Reconciliation after a period of conflict and exclusion is a beautiful thing. I hate the feelings surrounding conflict, and I love the feelings surrounding reconciliation.

In this section of Scripture, Paul details the worst kind of alienation—alienation from both God and others. Then he contrasts that with the infinite beauty surrounding our restoration. Once again, the first word of this section, *therefore*, reminds us that everything he says here builds on the spiritual blessings in Christ that he taught us in the last section—in particular that our salvation is by grace through faith, not of our own works, and we have nothing in which to boast. The humility that results from a correct understanding of Ephesians 2:1-10 is key to unlocking the rest of the chapter. Paul uses a clear progression of thought to make his point. He recounts what we used to be in verses 11-12, he emphasizes again what Christ has done for us in verses 13-18, and he reveals what we are now becoming in Christ in verses 19-22.

---

[22] Strongs, s. v. "appallotrioo."

Read through Ephesians 2:11 – 3:21. Note the words or phrases that stand out to you.

Ephesians 2

[11]Therefore remember that at one time you Gentiles in the flesh, called "the uncircumcision" by what is called the circumcision, which is made in the flesh by hands— [12]remember that you were at that time separated from Christ, alienated from the commonwealth of Israel and strangers to the covenants of promise, having no hope and without God in the world. [13]But now in Christ Jesus you who once were far off have been brought near by the blood of Christ. [14]For he himself is our peace, who has made us both one and has broken down in his flesh the dividing wall of hostility [15]by abolishing the law of commandments expressed in ordinances, that he might create in himself one new man in place of the two, so making peace, [16]and might reconcile us both to God in one body through the cross, thereby killing the hostility. [17]And he came and preached peace to you who were far off and peace to those who were near. [18]For through him we both have access in one Spirit to the Father. [19]So then you are no longer strangers and aliens, but you are fellow citizens with the saints and members of the household of God, [20]built on the foundation of the apostles and prophets, Christ Jesus himself being the cornerstone, [21]in whom the whole structure, being joined together, grows into a holy temple in the Lord. [22]In him you also are being built together into a dwelling place for God by the Spirit.

Ephesians 3

[1]For this reason I, Paul, a prisoner for Christ Jesus on behalf of you Gentiles—[2]assuming that you have heard of the stewardship of God's grace that was given to me for you, [3]how the mystery was made known to me by revelation, as I have written briefly. [4]When you read this, you can perceive my insight into the mystery of Christ, [5]which was not made known to the sons of men in other generations as it has now been revealed to his holy apostles and prophets by the Spirit. [6]This mystery is that the Gentiles are fellow heirs, members of the same body, and partakers of the promise in Christ Jesus through the gospel.

[7]Of this gospel I was made a minister according to the gift of God's grace, which was given me by the working of his power. [8]To me, though I am the very least of all the saints, this grace was given, to preach to the Gentiles the unsearchable riches of Christ, [9]and to bring to light for everyone what is the plan of the mystery hidden

for ages in God who created all things, [10]so that through the church the manifold wisdom of God might now be made known to the rulers and authorities in the heavenly places. [11]This was according to the eternal purpose that he has realized in Christ Jesus our Lord, [12]in whom we have boldness and access with confidence through our faith in him. [13]So I ask you not to lose heart over what I am suffering for you, which is your glory.

[14]For this reason I bow my knees before the Father, [15]from whom every family in heaven and on earth is named, [16]that according to the riches of his glory he may grant you to be strengthened with power through his Spirit in your inner being, [17]so that Christ may dwell in your hearts through faith—that you, being rooted and grounded in love, [18]may have strength to comprehend with all the saints what is the breadth and length and height and depth, [19]and to know the love of Christ that surpasses knowledge, that you may be filled with all the fullness of God.

[20]Now to him who is able to do far more abundantly than all that we ask or think, according to the power at work within us, [21]to him be glory in the church and in Christ Jesus throughout all generations, forever and ever. Amen.

Chapter 8   Ephesians 2:11-18

11 Therefore remember that at one time you Gentiles in the flesh, called "the uncircumcision" by what is called the circumcision, which is made in the flesh by hands— 12 remember that you were at that time separated from Christ, alienated from the commonwealth of Israel and strangers to the covenants of promise, having no hope and without God in the world. 13 But now in Christ Jesus you who once were far off have been brought near by the blood of Christ. 14 For he himself is our peace, who has made us both one and has broken down in his flesh the dividing wall of hostility 15 by abolishing the law of commandments expressed in ordinances, that he might create in himself one new man in place of the two, so making peace, 16 and might reconcile us both to God in one body through the cross, thereby killing the hostility. 17 And he came and preached peace to you who were far off and peace to those who were near. 18 For through him we both have access in one Spirit to the Father.

Separated, alienated, strangers

In verses 11-12, Paul reinforces what he has already presented in the first verses of chapter 2—the depth of our condition apart from God. This is one of at least three word pictures Paul uses in his epistles to show our need for God and our utter dependence on him to reach down to us. In Romans and Galatians, Paul speaks of us as slaves unable to free ourselves, bought out of slavery and adopted as God's own children. Earlier in Ephesians, he teaches that we are dead in our sins but made alive with and through Christ. Here Paul speaks of us as strangers and aliens—separated from those who have a covenant relationship with God; on the outside, looking in; longing for intimacy but unable to connect on our own.

This epistle was originally addressed to believers at the church in Ephesus. Formerly a colony of Greece, Ephesus was part of the Roman Empire at the time of Paul's writings. Ephesus was far away from Jerusalem and the surrounding areas of Jesus' earthly ministry. The people there were both physically and spiritually removed from the history of God's people that began in Genesis. To really understand their alienation from God and his children, we need to understand the "covenants of promise" to which they were strangers according to verse 12.

I have often heard it said that the Bible begins with a divorce and ends in a marriage, and everything in between is God wooing back his wayward Bride. That is a helpful way of looking at Scripture because it reflects the continuity of what God has been doing for his people throughout history. Some doctrinal traditions believe that God has worked with separate people groups throughout history and that what he did in the Old Testament with the nation of Israel is completely distinct from what he has done in the New Testament church through Christ. They believe that the church as we know it today began in Acts 2 at Pentecost. My concern with this view is that it reduces the Old Testament to a series of moral lessons with few doctrinal and theological links to today's church. This is a faulty way of looking at the continuity between the

Old and New Testament, and Paul addresses this multiple times in his writings (Romans 4, 9 –11, Galatians 3).

In Genesis 12 and 15, God came to Abraham and made what Paul calls in Ephesians the covenants of promise. At first reading, this covenant in Genesis does not sound like much, but we see later in the Old and New Testament that this covenant with Abraham is much bigger than it may appear at first. In Galatians 3:8, Paul calls the Genesis 12 account "preaching the gospel to Abraham beforehand." What is put forth in Genesis is an early taste of the good news—this covenant that God made with Abraham and his descendants even as he assumes both sides of the agreement, assuring its fulfillment by grace despite our failings.

God's chosen people are called different things throughout Scripture (the elect, the chosen, the Bride of Christ, the church, Israel). At some point in the New Testament, this group of God's chosen people were called Christians and their assembly referred to as the church. The evolution of the terms does not negate the consistent group to which each of these terms refers. In the Old Testament, they were called Israel and God's children. If we read the Old without referencing the New, we think the name Israel refers simply to the physical descendants of Abraham. Paul corrects this way of thinking in his writings, teaching that "not all Israel is Israel" (Romans 9:6). In other words, not all the physical descendants of Abraham are members of the true Israel. The true Israel (the true children of the promise) are those who BELIEVE God. Gentile believers are grafted into the vine of Israel. Physical Israelites who rejected God's promises concerning the Messiah are cut off (Romans 2:28-29). If this seems different than your beliefs, do not take my word on it. I encourage you to read (and wrestle) through Romans 2, 4, and 9-11 where Paul talks about this in depth.

All those who believed God's promises are part of one group of people--Christ's Body, the Elect, the Bride of Christ, the church. There is one distinct group of people that God has set his affection on throughout history, reflected in his covenant with Abraham and his descendents, and, to bring this back to the topic at hand, the people of Ephesus to which Paul writes were far removed from this group and their history.

Circumcision was the sign of God's covenant with Abraham. The label "uncircumcision" in Ephesians 2:11, given to Gentile believers by Jewish believers, was not merely a statement of fact but a derogatory reference to their outside-the-covenant status. The "in" crowd was the circumcision crowd. Those called the "uncircumcision" were alienated from the commonwealth of Israel and "strangers to the covenants of promise, having no hope and without God in the world." Wow. Their state was utterly hopeless.

But now in Christ Jesus

Like the phrase "But God" in Ephesians 2: 4, the wording here in verse 13 creates the same juxtaposition between the utter hopelessness of their state as detailed in verses 11-12 and the spiritual inheritance Paul has outlined in Ephesians 1. Now in Christ Jesus, everything has changed. We are no longer without hope in the world. We are no longer strangers to this covenant of promise.

According to verse 13, we have been "brought near by the blood of Christ." Brought near to what? Brought near to whom? This is the solution to the problem of verse 12. We were separated from Christ and far removed from him and his promises—but through his blood shed on the cross for our forgiveness, we are brought near to him. There is nothing worse than believing that there is a God but feeling far from him. As a long time Christian raised in gospel-believing churches, I still struggle with feeling that God is far away. Sometimes God is silent, but that does not mean he is not near. I have been brought near to God by the blood of Jesus. In Christ, I sit in God's throne room with constant access to his presence and ear. When I feel far from God, I have to meditate on this truth from Scripture. I stop and envision God in all his glory sitting on his throne as I sit at his feet gazing into his face. He may be silent for a time, but he is there! This is my heavenly reality.

Not only have we been brought near to Christ, but if we follow the outline of verse 12, we see we are also brought near to the commonwealth of Israel, God's chosen people, and the covenants of promise. Gentile believers had both vertical alienation from God and horizontal alienation from God's people. Now, through Christ's blood, we have what Charles Hodge calls a "double reconciliation." By fulfilling the demands of justice, Christ's death secured our reconciliation with God, and by abolishing the law in the form of the Mosaic ordinances, his death removed the wall of partition between the Jew and the Gentile.[23] Consider Galatians 3.

> 6 just as Abraham "believed God, and it was accounted to him for righteousness." 7 Therefore know that only those who are of faith are sons of Abraham. 8 And the Scripture, foreseeing that God would justify the Gentiles by faith, preached the gospel to Abraham beforehand, saying, "In you all the nations shall be blessed." 9 So then those who are of faith are blessed with believing Abraham. ...13 Christ has redeemed us from the curse of the law, having become a curse for us (for it is written, "Cursed is everyone who hangs on a tree"), 14 that the blessing of Abraham might come upon the Gentiles in Christ Jesus, that we might receive the promise of the Spirit through faith. ... 26 For you are all sons of God through faith in Christ Jesus. 27 For as many of you as were baptized into Christ have put on Christ. 28 There is neither Jew nor Greek, there is neither slave nor free, there is neither male nor female; for you are all one in Christ Jesus. 29 And if you are Christ's, then you are Abraham's seed, and heirs according to the promise.

In Galatians 3, Paul concludes by saying that we are now Abraham's seed and therefore heirs according to the promises God made to him.

I like the phrase Paul uses back in Ephesians 2:14, "he himself is our peace." Jesus did not just secure our peace or make a way for us to find peace. No, HE actually IS our peace. He broke down the wall of hostility, reconciling us to both God and the rest of the body of Christ. He brought peace to us by creating "in himself one new man in place of the two." He preached peace to those far off (the uncircumcision) and peace to those who were near (the circumcision), killing the hostility between us by his death on the cross.

In Ephesians 2:18, Paul says that both groups of believers now have free access to the Father in one Spirit. We are indwelt with the same Spirit that Christ promised to his disciples in John 15. Because of Christ's payment for our sins on the cross, the Spirit now serves as our direct link to God the Father in heaven himself. We now have direct access to God. Paul repeats this idea in Ephesians 3:12 as well.

---

[23] Charles Hodge, *Commentary on the Epistle to the Ephesians* (Wheaton, Ill: Crossway Books, 1994), 80-81.

in whom we have boldness and access with confidence through our faith in him.

The writer of Hebrews says it this way.

Hebrews 4:16 Let us then with confidence draw near to the throne of grace, that we may receive mercy and find grace to help in time of need.

Do you understand what great news this is? This is what makes the gospel at its purest form indeed GOOD NEWS. I love the implications of the words *boldly*, *confidence*, and throne of *grace* in Hebrews 4:16. First, we can *boldly* enter God's presence—not in fear of our lives as Esther entered the king's presence or afraid of a rebuke as many authority figures tend to give. Many of you had parents that did not receive your requests graciously. You learned to feel them out and tiptoe around their idiosyncrasies to protect yourself when you entered their presence. You had to brace yourself before walking into a room to ask them a question. Maybe you avoided the rooms they were in altogether because walking into their line of vision often invited criticism or abuse. The good news of the gospel is that this is NOT the character of your heavenly Father. You do not have to tiptoe around him, afraid you will set off his temper. You can walk into his presence boldly, with no hesitation or fear, and with confidence, fully trusting in the reliability of his promises to you.

Finally, the author of Hebrews refers to this place of access to the Father as the "throne of grace." Remember our exploration of grace in the first section? The hallmark attribute of God's throne room is GRACE—his loving kindness that we do not deserve and cannot earn. Here at this throne room characterized by his grace, we come to find the personal grace and mercy we need to make it through every situation. Come boldly, my sister! God has paid dearly through Christ's death on the cross to extend this invitation to you. His clear invitation is that you would come and avail yourself of this means of his grace.

Reflections

_____

_____

_____

_____

_____

_____

_____

_____

_____

_____

_____

Chapter 9 Ephesians 2:19-22

19 So then you are no longer strangers and aliens, but you are fellow citizens with the saints and members of the household of God, 20 built on the foundation of the apostles and prophets, Christ Jesus himself being the cornerstone, 21 in whom the whole structure, being joined together, grows into a holy temple in the Lord. 22 In him you also are being built together into a dwelling place for God by the Spirit.

No longer strangers, but fellow citizens

Paul uses multiple overlapping pictures to illustrate this new reconciliation we have with God and others. We used to be strangers and outcasts, but now we are fellow citizens of God's kingdom. We used to be orphans, but now we are members of God's own household. To be a member means that we are a distinct part of the whole.[24] It points both to our individuality as well as our unity, which Paul will discuss in more depth in Ephesians 4. Of what are we members? We are members or elemental parts of God's very own household. We live under his roof, and we are his family.

I saw a commercial recently for home furnishings that ended with a tagline along the lines, "Home is the most important place in the world." I have to fully agree with them. Home is our refuge. It is the base of our daily existence. It is the safe place to which we retreat when we are tired or sick. But I know that for many of you reading this, the word home evokes pain and longing, not peace and security. You may have a place to sleep, but it is not home in the true sense of the word. If that describes you, I want to emphasize to you, dear sister in Christ, that you DO have a home, and this world is not it. You have a home in the purest, most beautiful sense of the word. Find refuge and peace in God's promise to you that you are his family and that he maintains the eternal roof over your head.

Paul also illustrates our reconciliation to God and others with the picture of a dwelling place for God himself. The foundation, basis, and underpinnings are all God has taught us of himself and his plan through the prophets and apostles. The prophets spoke in the Old Testament and the apostles in the New. Their message together forms a coherent foundation for all God is doing for us through Christ now. Christ is the cornerstone, the essential, indispensable corner piece that seals the pieces of the building together. We are being built by the Holy Spirit into this structure, this holy temple that is God's dwelling place. This is the supernatural structure where God himself lives. What a beautiful picture Paul paints of all God is doing in and for us. Whatever our previous status was, we are now fully reconciled to God and others within his kingdom, his household, his Body, and his temple.

---

[24] *The American Heritage Dictionary of the English Language*, 4th ed., s. v. "member."

Reflections

Chapter 10 Ephesians 3:1-6

1 For this reason I, Paul, a prisoner for Christ Jesus on behalf of you Gentiles— 2 assuming that you have heard of the stewardship of God's grace that was given to me for you, 3 how the mystery was made known to me by revelation, as I have written briefly. 4 When you read this, you can perceive my insight into the mystery of Christ, 5 which was not made known to the sons of men in other generations as it has now been revealed to his holy apostles and prophets by the Spirit. 6 This mystery is that the Gentiles are fellow heirs, members of the same body, and partakers of the promise in Christ Jesus through the gospel.

This mystery

As we begin chapter 3 of Ephesians, Paul finally fully addresses the "mystery" to which he has referred several times already. As he regularly does in Ephesians, Paul opens this chapter with a connecting phrase, "for this reason." Once more, we are reminded that each teaching that Paul presents builds upon the last. In this case, the reason Paul is a prisoner for Christ on behalf of the Gentile believers at Ephesus is found in the closing of Ephesians 2—namely that the Gentiles are no longer strangers to God's promises but are now being built together with Jewish believers into a temple or dwelling place for God the Spirit.

Paul goes on to say that he has been a steward of God's grace given to him for Gentile believers. God has entrusted him with the message of the gospel to non-Jewish believers. This is the great mystery—"that the Gentiles are fellow heirs, members of the same body, and partakers of the promise in Christ Jesus through the gospel." Note that Paul says he is a prisoner on behalf of the Gentiles. Stott notes that "what had lead to his arrest in Jerusalem, his imprisonment there and in Caesarea, his successive trials and his subsequent appeal to Caesar which had brought him to Rome was fanatical Jewish opposition to his mission to the Gentiles."[25] Paul suffered much persecution to bring this mystery to light to the Gentiles.

The term mystery, which Paul uses repeatedly here and in other of his epistles, is the Greek word *musterion*.[26] It has a slightly different meaning than our English word mystery. In English, we think of a mystery as something dark, puzzling, and hard to be known. In contrast, the Greek word is simply a truth in which someone has been initiated, such as the initiation into a cult in which the mysteries of the cult are revealed. In Christianity, the mysteries are those truths we could not discover on our own but that God has now revealed openly to the whole church.[27] In

---

[25] Stott, p. 114.
[26] Strongs, s. v. "musterion."
[27] Stott, p. 116.

this case, the mystery is that God extends the good news of his salvation through Christ to non-Jewish believers.

Reflections

_____

_____

_____

_____

_____

_____

_____

_____

_____

_____

_____

_____

_____

_____

_____

_____

_____

_____

_____

_____

_____

_____

_____

_____

_____

_____

_____

Chapter 11 Ephesians 3: 7-13

7 Of this gospel I was made a minister according to the gift of God's grace, which was given me by the working of his power. 8 To me, though I am the very least of all the saints, this grace was given, to preach to the Gentiles the unsearchable riches of Christ, 9 and to bring to light for everyone what is the plan of the mystery hidden for ages in God who created all things, 10 so that through the church the manifold wisdom of God might now be made known to the rulers and authorities in the heavenly places. 11 This was according to the eternal purpose that he has realized in Christ Jesus our Lord, 12 in whom we have boldness and access with confidence through our faith in him. 13 So I ask you not to lose heart over what I am suffering for you, which is your glory.

The very least of all the saints

In verses 7-13, Paul gets personal. We get insight into how he feels about the ministry he has been given to the Gentiles that he has been articulating throughout Ephesians. According to the gift of God's grace and the working of his power, Paul is a minister of the gospel. The same Greek word for minister is also translated deacon and servant elsewhere in the New Testament.[28] Paul is entrusted as a steward with a great errand for the king. Look at how he views himself on this journey.

First, he is humble. He understands that he was not chosen because of his great gifts or engaging personality. He has a right assessment of himself. He is the "very least of all the saints." He echoes this I Tim. 1:13-16.

13 though formerly I was a blasphemer, persecutor, and insolent opponent. But I received mercy because I had acted ignorantly in unbelief, 14 and the grace of our Lord overflowed for me with the faith and love that are in Christ Jesus. 15 The saying is trustworthy and deserving of full acceptance, that Christ Jesus came into the world to save sinners, of whom I am the foremost. 16 But I received mercy for this reason, that in me, as the foremost, Jesus Christ might display his perfect patience as an example to those who were to believe in him for eternal life.

In reality, Paul has been entrusted with possibly the greatest message ever communicated. But instead of becoming puffed up with self-importance as so many of us do when entrusted with a great stewardship, he keeps an accurate assessment of himself. He is a good model for us here. He is not dwelling in self-condemnation. He is not insecure, searching for compliments to make him feel better about himself. Instead, he gets both the depth of his sin and the great grace that God has poured out on him. Tim Keller in *The Reason for God* puts it this way.

---

[28] Strongs, s. v. "diakonos."

The Christian gospel is that I am so flawed that Jesus had to die for me, yet I am so loved and valued that Jesus was glad to die for me. This leads to deep humility and deep confidence at the same time. It undermines both swaggering and sniveling. I cannot feel superior to anyone, and yet I have nothing to prove to anyone. I do not think more of myself nor less of myself. Instead, I think of myself less.[29]

Paul is first humble and second overflowing with excited confidence. He is preaching the unsearchable riches of Christ! He is bringing to light to everyone this mystery that has been hidden for ages. Through this message, the manifold or multi-faceted wisdom of God will be made known throughout the heavenly places, and this is all in accord with God's plans from before time began.

The wisdom of God made known to rulers and authorities in the heavenly places

I value the opportunities I have on earth in which my suffering can give testimony to God's great worth. If I am sick in the hospital, I can see some kingdom value to it if I am able to point nurses, doctors, or family to Christ. My problem comes when my suffering seems to have no earthly impact. No one seems to notice my faith. Perhaps I feel misunderstood by the very people I would like to influence. Maybe the entire trial seems contradictory to God's glory. Where is the value in earthly suffering if there is no positive kingdom testimony attached to it here on earth?

Paul teaches that there is a much more important battle for God's glory going on than what we can see on earth. This is first revealed in Scripture in the story of Job. Job's trials are on earth, but Job's faithfulness was lost on his family and friends. It was, however, not lost in the heavenly places. Satan's accusation was that Job only served God because God blessed him. But Job proved to Satan that God deserved obedience not because of his blessings on his children but simply because of whom he is. Job's three friends never figured it out, but Satan did. The Lord gives. The Lord takes away. Regardless, blessed be the name of the Lord, for he alone is worthy.

Paul says here in Ephesians that his suffering, while certainly meaningful and relevant on earth, was playing out on a much larger stage with heavenly witnesses. The final phrase from this section reminds us why the reality of what's happening in the heavenly places is so important to both Paul and the Ephesian believers. At that very moment, Paul on earth was suffering great persecution in jail as a result of his ministry to Gentile believers, and the Ephesian believers were close to losing heart. There was a stark contrast between their heavenly reality in Christ and the earthly reality they were experiencing in that moment. Paul understands all that is being done in the heavenly places, and his perspective on the persecution he is now enduring comes from his understanding of God's purposes from before time began playing themselves out in Ephesus, Corinth, Rome, Thessalonica, Colossi, and Philippi. These believers' faithfulness in persecution was the very thing that silenced heavenly critics by what they reflected of the character and worth of God.

---

[29] Tim Keller, *The Reason for God* (New York: Dutton Publishers, 2008), 181.

Chapter 12 Ephesians 3:14-21

14 For this reason I bow my knees before the Father, 15 from whom every family in heaven and on earth is named, 16 that according to the riches of his glory he may grant you to be strengthened with power through his Spirit in your inner being, 17 so that Christ may dwell in your hearts through faith—that you, being rooted and grounded in love, 18 may have strength to comprehend with all the saints what is the breadth and length and height and depth, 19 and to know the love of Christ that surpasses knowledge, that you may be filled with all the fullness of God.

To know the love that surpasses knowledge

Now that I understand Paul's heart that the believers at Ephesus connect his earthly suffering in prison with the reality of all God is doing in the heavenly places, his final exhortation at the end of Ephesians 3 takes on new meaning. It moves me deeply. Paul is in jail, soon to be executed, pouring himself out in prayer for the hearts of those for whom he is being persecuted. Paul has soaked in the message of God's grace, and it has penetrated him at a soul-deep level. It has given him perspective on all that he is enduring, and now his prayer is that the Ephesians would get it at a soul-deep level too.

Paul wants the Ephesians (and you and I) to be profoundly moved by the immeasurable riches of the grace of God through Christ Jesus. He wants us to comprehend the breadth, length, height, and depth of God's love—a love that really surpasses our ability to grasp. I am amused and intrigued by the phrasing in verse 19 that he wants us to comprehend something beyond our comprehension, to know something that surpasses knowledge. But Paul's example is helpful here. When I contrast what I know of Paul's earthly reality with his sincere joy, peace, and enthusiasm for his heavenly reality, I am moved by something that is beyond my ability to fully comprehend.

Paul closes Ephesians 3 with the two verses that are, at least in my experience, the most used to close services in the history of the church. In church liturgy, we call it the benediction—Latin for a good saying—that final exhortation before we leave our church services to go reengage with the world.

20 Now to him who is able to do far more abundantly than all that we ask or think, according to the power at work within us, 21 to him be glory in the church and in Christ Jesus throughout all generations, forever and ever. Amen.

This good word at the end of chapter three is also the ending to this second section of Ephesians. Paul is closing his thoughts on this mystery now revealed of God's double reconciliation of Gentile believers to both himself and Jewish believers. His final reflection is on the glory of God through Christ and his church. God is doing far more than we realize, far more than we are even able to comprehend. The power that is doing all of these things is the same power at work within us now, and this thing he is now doing through Christ and the church is for his glory through all generations for all time. Let us stop with Paul and the Ephesian believers for a moment and praise God's holy name for revealing to us this great plan he has to reconcile Jew and Gentile to himself, for he is worthy.

Reflections

_____
_____
_____
_____
_____
_____
_____
_____
_____
_____
_____
_____
_____
_____
_____
_____
_____
_____
_____
_____
_____
_____
_____
_____

Section 3 Ephesians 4:1– 5:21

When I finished writing the first draft of section 2, I was both emotionally drained and passionately motivated. I was moved by how Paul's understanding of his heavenly reality empowered him to deal with his earthly reality and even to encourage others despite his own poor conditions under house arrest. Things were not going well for Paul on earth, and they continued downward from the time he wrote Ephesians to his death not long afterwards. But Paul had something in Christ that transformed how he viewed his earthly circumstances. I hope you too grasp with Paul the importance of our spiritual reality and how a correct understanding of it transforms how we view the good and the bad in our daily lives.

It is important that we cling diligently to the hope of the unsearchable riches we have in Christ as we move into Ephesians 4. Now Paul starts to get really practical. He shows us how our spiritual reality in heaven breaks into our physical reality on earth—how it transforms how we think about each other on earth and equips us to choose radically different responses to circumstances that bring so many people down.

Read through Ephesians 4:1 – 5:21. Note the words or phrases that stand out to you.

Ephesians 4

[1]I therefore, a prisoner for the Lord, urge you to walk in a manner worthy of the calling to which you have been called, [2]with all humility and gentleness, with patience, bearing with one another in love, [3]eager to maintain the unity of the Spirit in the bond of peace. [4]There is one body and one Spirit—just as you were called to the one hope that belongs to your call— [5]one Lord, one faith, one baptism, [6]one God and Father of all, who is over all and through all and in all. [7]But grace was given to each one of us according to the measure of Christ's gift. [8]Therefore it says,

> "When he ascended on high he led a host of captives,
>   and he gave gifts to men."

[9](In saying, "He ascended," what does it mean but that he had also descended into the lower regions, the earth? [10]He who descended is the one who also ascended far above all the heavens, that he might fill all things.) [11]And he gave the apostles, the prophets, the evangelists, the shepherds and teachers, [12]to equip the saints for the work of ministry, for building up the body of Christ, [13]until we all attain to the unity of the faith and of the knowledge of the Son of God, to mature manhood, to the measure of the stature of the fullness of Christ, [14]so that we may no longer be children, tossed to and fro by the waves and carried about by every wind of doctrine, by human cunning, by craftiness in deceitful schemes. [15]Rather, speaking the truth in love, we are to grow up in every way into him who is the head, into Christ, [16]from whom the whole body, joined and held together by every joint with which it is equipped, when each part is working properly, makes the body grow so that it builds itself up in love.

[17]Now this I say and testify in the Lord, that you must no longer walk as the Gentiles do, in the futility of their minds. [18]They are darkened in their understanding, alienated from the life of God because of the ignorance that is in them, due to their hardness of heart. [19]They have become callous and have given themselves up to sensuality, greedy to practice every kind of impurity. [20]But that is not the way you learned Christ!— [21]assuming that you have heard about him and were taught in him, as the truth is in Jesus, [22]to put

off your old self, which belongs to your former manner of life and is corrupt through deceitful desires, [23]and to be renewed in the spirit of your minds, [24]and to put on the new self, created after the likeness of God in true righteousness and holiness.

[25]Therefore, having put away falsehood, let each one of you speak the truth with his neighbor, for we are members one of another. [26]Be angry and do not sin; do not let the sun go down on your anger, [27]and give no opportunity to the devil. [28]Let the thief no longer steal, but rather let him labor, doing honest work with his own hands, so that he may have something to share with anyone in need. [29]Let no corrupting talk come out of your mouths, but only such as is good for building up, as fits the occasion, that it may give grace to those who hear. [30]And do not grieve the Holy Spirit of God, by whom you were sealed for the day of redemption. [31]Let all bitterness and wrath and anger and clamor and slander be put away from you, along with all malice. [32]Be kind to one another, tenderhearted, forgiving one another, as God in Christ forgave you.

Ephesians 5

[1]Therefore be imitators of God, as beloved children. [2]And walk in love, as Christ loved us and gave himself up for us, a fragrant offering and sacrifice to God.

[3]But sexual immorality and all impurity or covetousness must not even be named among you, as is proper among saints. [4]Let there be no filthiness nor foolish talk nor crude joking, which are out of place, but instead let there be thanksgiving. [5]For you may be sure of this, that everyone who is sexually immoral or impure, or who is covetous (that is, an idolater), has no inheritance in the kingdom of Christ and God. [6]Let no one deceive you with empty words, for because of these things the wrath of God comes upon the sons of disobedience. [7]Therefore do not become partners with them; [8]for at one time you were darkness, but now you are light in the Lord. Walk as children of light [9](for the fruit of light is found in all that is good and right and true), [10]and try to discern what is pleasing to the Lord. [11]Take no part in the unfruitful works of darkness, but instead expose them. [12]For it is shameful even to speak of the things that they do in secret. [13]But when anything is exposed by the light, it becomes visible, [14]for anything that becomes visible is light. Therefore it says,

"Awake, O sleeper,
and arise from the dead,
and Christ will shine on you."

[15]Look carefully then how you walk, not as unwise but as wise, [16]making the best use of the time, because the days are evil. [17]Therefore do not be foolish, but understand what the will of the Lord is. [18]And do not get drunk with wine, for that is debauchery, but be filled with the Spirit, [19]addressing one another in psalms and hymns and spiritual songs, singing and making melody to the Lord with your heart, [20]giving thanks always and for everything to God the Father in the name of our Lord Jesus Christ, [21]submitting to one another out of reverence for Christ.

Chapter 13 Ephesians 4: 1-3

1 I therefore, a prisoner for the Lord, urge you to walk in a manner worthy of the calling to which you have been called, 2 with all humility and gentleness, with patience, bearing with one another in love, 3 eager to maintain the unity of the Spirit in the bond of peace.

Therefore

Again, Paul is clearly linking his exhortation here to what he has already presented of the spiritual blessings we have in Christ in the heavenly places and, in particular, the mystery that he has just explained to us of the reconciliation of Gentile believers to both God and others in the Body of Christ. He refers to himself here as a prisoner for the Lord, reminding his readers that he has earned the right to speak boldly to them. Paul now speaks with unflinching honesty, saying that if you want to walk in a way that accurately reflects the doctrine he just outlined, then you will do several very specific things. You will be humble, gentle, patient, and loving for the long haul with others in the Body of Christ. You will be eager to maintain the unity of the Spirit. We will now unpack these phrases and meditate on the high calling we have in Christ.

Walk in a manner worthy

What kind of manner is worthy of the calling Paul has articulated in Ephesians 1-3? In other words, what kind of day-to-day responses befit the value of our spiritual inheritance in Christ? This is a place to park for a while. My parents became Christians shortly after I was born and raised me in gospel-believing churches. I have decades of experience in churches and conservative Christianity in general. However, I noted during my time in conservative churches and working for various Christian organizations that many Christians can articulate the gospel and their calling in Christ Jesus, but they do not go on to make the connection that Paul does to walking daily in a way that reflects well on the worth of this calling. When well-meaning Christians are not diligent to walk forward in unity, it reflects very poorly on the gospel. There is a long history of people rejecting the Christian faith for this very reason. Why believe the gospel when God's people respond to each other in ways that mock the reconciliation we have with God and each other in Christ?!

I admit that this particular teaching of Paul has impacted me a great deal personally. As I mentioned before, I have witnessed much acrimony over the years among people who all claimed to believe the same gospel Paul outlines in Ephesians 1 and 2. I remember reading Ephesians 4 along with Jesus' similar teaching in John 17 when I was newly married. At the time I was perplexed. Jesus' prayer in John 17 is that his followers would be unified the way the Trinity is unified in order that we accurately reflect the gospel. In contrast, the rhetoric I was hearing in my Christian circles emphasized why this or that other Christian group was wrong and why we could not fellowship with them. I was taught that it was more important to separate from and not be identified with another Christian group than it was to pursue unity with them. When I read Jesus' words in John 17 and Paul's words in Ephesians 4, I was confronted with a Biblical instruction that was very different from my Christian experience. I was tempted to doubt Jesus' words. Surely if Jesus really meant his instructions the way I was reading them, the Christians I knew would be more diligent to pursue unity and not so eager to break away from someone. It took a long time before I came to accept that Jesus and Paul both meant exactly what they said at face value. I am tempted to get on a soapbox and lecture against all I have witnessed, but then I would likely be violating the very thing Paul is advocating. Instead, I want to study Paul's positive example as our model rather than highlighting all the ways Christians have failed to obey these instructions throughout church history.

We must note that the foundation of Paul's instructions is a correct understanding of the gospel. This is not about pursuing unity with people who believe a different gospel. This is about unity with fellow believers—all those who are IN CHRIST with all the reconciliation to God and others implied by that phrase. What responses are worthy of the true gospel?

Humility

I was taken back a bit when I first read the definition of the Greek term translated humility. It means a deep sense of your littleness, especially your moral littleness.[30] Unlike our culture's watered down version of this term, humility does not mean that you are simply nice, polite, or diplomatic. It means that you have a correct understanding of your salvation as Paul outlined in Ephesians 2. You understand that you were dead in your sins, you were born a child deserving of God's judgment, and God saved you by his grace and not by your own good works. You understand your moral littleness. Then you respond to others in light of this understanding. A humble person does not stand in judgment against others from a point of righteous indignation. You and I have completely missed the entire message of Ephesians 1 and 2 if we think we have any moral high ground over anyone else. This is at the core of the gospel.

Another aspect of the definition of humility involves the concept of lowliness. Jesus is our living example throughout the gospels. Consider the magnificent description of Christ from Colossians 1.

> 15 He is the image of the invisible God, the firstborn over all creation. 16 For by him all things were created: things in heaven and on earth, visible and invisible, whether thrones or powers or rulers or authorities; all things were created by him and for him. 17 He is before all things, and in him all things hold together. 18 And he is the head of the body, the church; he is the beginning and the firstborn from among the dead, so that in everything he might have the supremacy.

Contrast that with the humility Jesus lived out for us and calls us to repeat in Philippians 2.

---

[30] Strongs, s. v. "tapeinophrosune."

5 Your attitude should be the same as that of Christ Jesus: 6 Who, being in very nature God, did not consider equality with God something to be grasped, 7 but made himself nothing, taking the very nature of a servant, being made in human likeness. 8 And being found in appearance as a man, he humbled himself and became obedient to death—even death on a cross!

As I meditate on the example of Christ, lowering himself to be born in a manger, to wash the feet of his disciples, and to die in such a shameful way before the very people he came to save, I understand why God repeats in Proverbs, James, and I Peter that God resists the proud but gives grace to the humble. That is a profound statement. God is firmly set against the actions of the proud—those who have an inflated view of their own merits and look down on others accordingly. He resists them. Why? Because humility and pride are key responses that indicate you either do or do not get the gospel and that we either are or are not being conformed to the image of Christ. May we be a humble people, not with simple politeness and sham diplomacy that masquerades as authentic humility, but with the genuine heart of a servant, esteeming others better than ourselves and letting go of our rights for the cause of Christ. May we be like Jesus.

Gentleness

The term gentleness implies not weakness but true strength under control. There are two extremes of character that are equally destructive and unhelpful in the Body of Christ. The first are weak people—doormats. Consider the Apostle Paul's reference to weak-willed women in 2 Timothy 3.

6 For among them are those who creep into households and capture weak women, burdened with sins and led astray by various passions,

Despite widespread misconceptions that authentic Christianity teaches women to be weak, Scripture never teaches weakness as a valued Christian character trait for men or women. But the opposite is equally destructive in the Body of Christ. Strong people whose strength is not under the control of the Spirit tear apart the Body of Christ. In contrast to both weakness and uncontrolled strength, gentleness is distinct from each. Our culture often confuses gentleness with weakness. A baby is weak. In contrast, an adult is gentle when they have the strength to crush the baby but instead temper that strength to cradle it.

God's people who walk worthy of their calling in Christ are known by their tempered strength. They are approachable and moderate. While they are quite strong, they do not use their strength to wound others but are humble and gentle with Jesus as their model.

Patience

Patience is a well-known Christian virtue, and I have heard it discussed many times during my years in the church. I have thrown out the term to others as others have to me. As so often is the case, I was moved out of complacency when I began studying the Greek term for patience.

Reading the definition in the Greek intensified the power of what Paul is teaching us here. The Greek word is *makrothumia*, and it means endurance, steadfastness, perseverance, longsuffering, and slowness in avenging wrongs.[31] I am convicted simply reading the definition.

If we are going to walk in a manner worthy of the gospel and all we have in Christ, we will endure for the long haul with fellow believers. We will be steadfast people that others can count on. We will persevere in relationships and be slow in avenging wrongs. We will suffer long with others and in so doing, reflect the truth of the reconciliation we have with God and others through Jesus Christ.

Bearing with one another in love

This phrase is the one in this section that has rattled around in my head the most lately. It sums up the other characteristics we just discussed. During my many years in Christianity, I have seen the opposite of this characteristic probably more than any other. Believers give up on each other, write each other off, stop calling or emailing, and just walk away. Many times, I have been the one who copped out—who stopped calling or caring or pursuing because the person in question got too complicated. God has convicted me on this issue personally in the last year. What exactly does this phrase mean and what does it look like practically?

The Greek word translated *bearing* means to sustain, bear, endure, or tolerate.[32] The New American Standard translates this phrase "showing tolerance" for other believers. We are called to tolerate other believers—to put up with Christians. The language here implies enduring even when someone invites scorn or repudiation. This is not the language of smooth sailing with others as we cheerfully pursue the same goals in harmony. This phrase implies overcoming some type of adversity or negativity. It assumes there is conflict.

The final phrase, *in love*, intensifies this instruction. We do not just endure with a grimace because we have no choice. We endure and tolerate in the spirit of love. But even the term *love* has lost its meaning in our culture. Thankfully, God tells us in I Corinthians 13 exactly what he means when he uses the term. Let's review God's definition of love for a moment.

> 4 Love is patient and kind; love does not envy or boast; it is not arrogant 5 or rude. It does not insist on its own way; it is not irritable or resentful; 6 it does not rejoice at wrongdoing, but rejoices with the truth. 7 Love bears all things, believes all things, hopes all things, endures all things.

Combining Paul's teaching from Ephesians 4 with his teaching in I Corinthians 13, we see that to reflect well on the gospel we must tolerate, endure, and bear long with others with genuine patience, kindness, and humility. Pride, rudeness, irritation, and resentment are all inconsistent with this instruction. We do not rejoice in another's downfall but stick with them, believing in them and hoping the best for them. We endure with them.

When I finally grasped what Paul was teaching here, my first reaction was to protest against all the ways I have seen this principle violated over the years in my Christian circles. It has only been in the last few years that I have started to understand that change begins with ME. When I

---

[31] Strongs, s. v. "makrothumia."
[32] Ibid, s. v. "anechomai."

examined my own life, I realized I was more committed to this in public than I was in private. What does it look like for me personally to walk in a manner worthy of my calling? In the conflicts that hit me closest to home, do I humbly, gently bear long in love? Who is it that I need to tolerate with patience? Whose burdens do I need to bear even though it is not convenient to do so? It is probably the person on whom you are most tempted to give up who most needs your phone call, email, or visit today.

For me, my home is ground zero on this issue. Sometimes, the people that are hardest to bear long in loving tolerance are my own family. Bearing long in love with my husband and children has been the best practice for doing it with others in the Body of Christ. My husband, children, and I often live together in wonderful, supportive accord. But there are definitely moments when grace is needed—sometimes weeks, months, or years at a time. I watch the light of the gospel shine brightly in our home when I respond with loving tolerance, endurance, patience, and humility when relationships are strained, and I watch it dim when I choose to alienate or repudiate my loved ones when times get tough.

I have noticed that I want grace to be circular. But that is not the nature of grace and Biblical love. If I am waiting on someone to show me grace before I show it to them, or if I only show someone else grace expecting them to respond in kind, then I have missed the entire point. The point of forbearing love is that the other person did NOT extend grace and love to me. If they had, I would not be showing them tolerance. I would just be responding in kind. Forbearing love begins with ME. I must be the first person to show it in the midst of ungracious responses toward me.

Eager to maintain the unity of the Spirit

This unity is created by God and is precious to him. He bought it with his blood and has nurtured his plan for our unity since before time began. The Spirit is the force in each of our hearts that unifies us in Christ, and we are called to eagerly maintain this unity.

The Greek word for *eager* means to exert oneself or give diligently toward a goal. It can also be translated to *make every effort.*[33] The Greek word for *maintain* means to take care of, to attend to carefully, and to guard.[34] The term *maintain* points to the fact that the Spirit has already created this unity that we are now called to support and encourage. I find looking up the definitions of such words very helpful. If I can say the same thing several different ways, it tends to emphasize the meaning so I do not forget it. In this case, we are called to make every effort to guard this unity. We are to exert ourselves willingly to the care of this unity. We are to give ourselves diligently to its preservation.

I will sum up this section on our need to diligently pursue and preserve unity in the Body of Christ with a quote from Stott on humility.

Now humility is essential to unity. Pride lurks behind all discord, while the greatest single secret of concord is humility. It is not difficult to prove this in experience. The people we immediately, instinctively like, and find it easy to get on with, are the people who give us the respect we consider we

---

[33] Strongs, s. v. "spoudazo."
[34] Ibid, s. v. "tereo."

deserve, while the people we immediately, instinctively dislike are those who treat us like dirt. In other words, personal vanity is a key factor in all our relationships. If, however, instead of maneuvering for the respect of others (which is pride) we give them our respect by recognizing their intrinsic God-given worth (which is humility), we shall be promoting harmony in God's new society.[35]

Reflections

_____

_____

_____

_____

_____

_____

_____

_____

_____

_____

_____

_____

_____

_____

_____

_____

_____

_____

_____

_____

_____

_____

_____

_____

_____

_____

_____

[35] Stott, p. 148-149.

Chapter 14 Ephesians 4: 4-6

4 There is one body and one Spirit—just as you were called to the one hope that belongs to your call— 5 one Lord, one faith, one baptism, 6 one God and Father of all, who is over all and through all and in all.

One body

Here it is the great summary of why you must eagerly pursue unity with other believers despite all the dysfunction you have likely witnessed in your church experience—because there is only ONE Body. Paul is talking about the Body of Christ, which is made up of all those Christ has reconciled to himself—i. e. the Church. How do you define the Church? It is not church membership or denominational status, nor is it the building or the programs. What Paul is talking about here is simply all those who are IN CHRIST as he has described in Ephesians 1-3. The church is the people—not the building, the programs, the denominational bylaws, or the membership roles. You and I have an obligation that extends well beyond the boundaries of our particular "church." We have an organic union with all those who are in Christ no matter where or when they lived. All believers, past, present, and future make up one Body. The ramifications of Paul's point here are extensive.

The Church is notoriously unlovable. Consider again the picture of God's people painted in the book of Hosea. By God's own order, Hosea marries the harlot Gomer and has a child with her. She then has two other children with different men. Hosea takes her and her children back despite her adultery. Gomer leaves him again, returns to harlotry, and eventually becomes a slave. Hosea buys her back in public auction and brings her home, not as his slave, but again as his wife. God uses Hosea's life story as a picture of his pursuit of his own people. God's people have broken their covenant with him throughout history. In return, God has relentlessly pursued his people, the Church, not because of her beauty or worthiness but for his own glory. As Paul said in Ephesians 1, God has lavished his love on us to the praise of his glorious grace. He is sanctifying his Church, rooting out her sin, and transforming her into the beautiful bride that he will present to Jesus at the marriage supper of the lamb in Revelation.

God is certainly doing a beautiful thing in and through his people. The Church will one day be presented spotless before God. But she is not there yet. The Church is a mess. This should make sense to us since she is made up completely of individuals who are all messes. The problem with the Church is that you and I are in it! Each of us in Jesus' Body were by nature children deserving of God's wrath. Each of us has no righteousness to offer God on our own. Each of us was saved by God's grace and not our good works which Isaiah likened to filthy menstrual rags (Isaiah 64:6). It is important that we have a Biblically informed understanding of just who exactly the Body of

Christ, the Church, is. If we do not, we are going to be disappointed and disillusioned, likely to the point that we give up on the whole idea altogether.

However, if we understand the Church, both the good and the bad, as Scripture presents her, then when she fails us, we understand that this is just her nature. We fight for unity in her anyway because we know she is Jesus' Body. There is a great line from a song by Derek Webb in which he sings as Christ would about his church. "You can not live for me with no regard for her. If you love me you will love my church."[36]

You cannot say to Jesus, "I like your Head, but your Body disgusts me." It is his BODY. God chose this picture to communicate to us something deep and beautiful about his people. We are one with each other and one with Christ. Therefore, we have to deal with the Church. We cannot cut ourselves off from her and expect a healthy relationship with Christ. It is all one glorious, supernatural entity. To believe the gospel means that we are in Christ, and to be in Christ means that we are supernaturally connected to his Body. Therefore, to reflect well on the gospel, we must diligently pursue unity with his Body for we are ONE.

Reflections

_____
_____
_____
_____
_____
_____
_____
_____
_____
_____
_____
_____
_____
_____
_____
_____
_____
_____

---

[36] Webb, Derek. "The Church." *She Must and Shall Go Free.* INO Records, 2003.

Chapter 15 Ephesians 4: 7-12

7 But grace was given to each one of us according to the measure of Christ's gift. 8 Therefore it says,
    "When he ascended on high he led a host of captives,
      and he gave gifts to men."
9 (In saying, "He ascended," what does it mean but that he had also descended into the lower regions, the earth? 10 He who descended is the one who also ascended far above all the heavens, that he might fill all things.) 11 And he gave the apostles, the prophets, the evangelists, the shepherds and teachers, 12 to equip the saints for the work of ministry, for building up the body of Christ, ...

But grace was given to each one of us

Notice the contrast between verses 4-6 and verse 7. In verses 4-6, Paul speaks repeatedly of the unity we have in Christ. There is one body, one Spirit, one hope, one Lord, one faith, one baptism, and one God weaving us all together. Then in verse 7, Paul switches from talking about the Body of Christ as a collective whole and draws attention instead to each of us individually.

(Paul) is, in fact, deliberately qualifying what he has just written about the church's unity. Although there is only one body, one faith and one family, this unity is not to be misconstrued as a lifeless or colorless uniformity ... On the contrary, the unity of the church, far from being boringly monotonous, is exciting in its diversity. This is not just because of our different cultures, temperaments and personalities (which, though true, is not Paul's point here), but because of the different gifts which Christ distributes for the enrichment of our common life.[37]

Each of us who are in Christ has been blessed with a grace gift—gifts of God's grace to accomplish the particular works he has planned in advance for each of us to do. Paul talks about these gifts in more detail in Romans 12 and I Corinthians 12-14. In Romans 12, Paul repeats many of the ideas he has put forth in Ephesians.

3 For by the grace given me I say to every one of you: Do not think of yourself more highly than you ought, but rather think of yourself with sober judgment, in accordance with the measure of faith God has given you. 4 Just as each of us has one body with many members, and these members do not all have the same function, 5 so in Christ we who are many form one body, and each member belongs to all the others. 6 We have different gifts, according to the grace given us. If a man's gift is prophesying, let him use it in proportion to his faith. 7 If it is serving, let him serve; if it is teaching, let him teach; 8 if it is encouraging, let him encourage; if it is contributing to the needs of others, let him give generously; if it is leadership, let him govern diligently; if it is showing mercy, let him do it cheerfully. 9 Love must be

---

[37] Stott, p. 155.

73

...at is evil; cling to what is good. 10 Be devoted to one another in brotherly love. Honor ...ove yourselves.

...this passage in Romans by emphasizing humility and ends his discussion with the ...of love. He gives a similar exhortation in I Corinthians 12-14, except there he parks on ...essity of love for an entire chapter.

...Ephesians 4:10, Paul highlights specific gifts that have the common element of proclaiming doctrine—apostles, prophets, evangelists, shepherds, and teachers. The Romans passage highlights an entirely different set of gifts. In each passage that lists particular gifts, the lists overlap but do not repeat exactly, suggesting that there is not an exhaustive list of the gifts of the Spirit. These gifts are varied and valuable. More important than analyzing the nuances of a particular grace gift is grasping God's clearly stated purpose for these gifts—"to equip the saints for the work of the ministry, the building up of the Body of Christ." In every place that Scripture talks about such gifts, the foundational purpose of gifts is always loving, sacrificial service that builds up the Body of Christ toward mature unity.

Another point to note here is that while we traditionally refer to this concept as the gifts of the Spirit, in Ephesians 4 the gifts are from Christ and Romans 12 points to God the Father as the origin of these gifts. It is wise to note the participation of each member of the Trinity in this gifting of grace.

He led a host of captives

In the middle of this section are two verses that might seem random and out of place.

8 Therefore it says,
  "When he ascended on high he led a host of captives,
  and he gave gifts to men."
9 (In saying, "He ascended," what does it mean but that he had also descended into the lower regions, the earth? 10 He who descended is the one who also ascended far above all the heavens, that he might fill all things.)

These verses speak of the ascension of Christ and actually have significant relevance to this section on the giving of gifts by Christ. These verses highlight the authority and supremacy of Christ, his right to give such gifts, and his power to sustain those gifts in us.

Paul is quoting Psalms 68, in which the psalmist praises God as the supreme conqueror of all authorities.

18 You ascended on high,
  leading a host of captives in your train
  and receiving gifts among men,
  even among the rebellious, that the LORD God may dwell there.

If you are like me, your next question is who is this host of captives following Jesus in his ascension? Colossians 2:15 sheds some light on this.

He disarmed the rulers and authorities and put them to open shame, by triumphing over them in him.

We already know from our study of the closing of Ephesians 1 that God has seated Christ in the heavenly places "far above all rule and authority and power and dominion, and above every name that is named, not only in this age but also in the one to come" (v. 21). Furthermore, God has placed "all things under his feet" (v. 22). So the picture in Ephesians 4: 8-9 is of Christ ascending in triumph with all other authorities trailing in his wake, submitted to his will. This is the Christ that is gifting us with his grace for ministry to his Body—supremely powerful ruler of all.

Reflections

_____
_____
_____
_____
_____
_____
_____
_____
_____
_____
_____
_____
_____
_____
_____
_____
_____
_____
_____
_____
_____
_____

Chapter 16 Ephesians 4: 13-16

13 until we all attain to the unity of the faith and of the knowledge of the Son of God, to mature manhood, to the measure of the stature of the fullness of Christ, 14 so that we may no longer be children, tossed to and fro by the waves and carried about by every wind of doctrine, by human cunning, by craftiness in deceitful schemes. 15 Rather, speaking the truth in love, we are to grow up in every way into him who is the head, into Christ, 16 from whom the whole body, joined and held together by every joint with which it is equipped, when each part is working properly, makes the body grow so that it builds itself up in love.

Unity of the faith, knowledge of the Son of God, and mature manhood

In dealing with our Christian community, it is essential we keep our eye on the prize—the end result of the Body of Christ growing together in unity and maturity in the true knowledge of God. As the daughter of a cotton farmer, I remember a farming illustration I heard growing up. If a farmer wanted to plow a straight line for a row of crops, he needed to keep his eye on a fixed point at the end of the row. If he looked down where he was, he would make a crooked line. But if he kept his eye on the spot that he wanted to reach at the end, he would maintain a straight line for his row of crops. This is a helpful illustration for us as we deal with issues and relationships within the Body of Christ, the Church. We have to keep our eye on the goal. What is the end result of all God is doing now? It is a church that is unified in the faith and the knowledge of God, measuring up to the stature of Christ. God is moving us toward the goal of Christian maturity in which we are no longer weak Christians easily deceived by every new doctrinal error. We will be a Body that works together in harmony and unity, each part doing its job. And what does fully realized Christian maturity look like? It looks like Christ (v. 13)!

As we discussed before, the Church is NOT there yet, but God calls us to choose the proper place to fix our focus. He calls us to focus squarely on the goal to which he is conforming his Body. We are not to focus on all the ways the Church fails him and us now. I am not suggesting we stick our head in the sand and ignore her failings. That is not Christian unity either. But I am saying that our perspective on the current failings of the Church must be informed by the end result that God promises he will accomplish—a beautiful, mature Body steadfast in correct doctrine where members work together and support each other. Knowing where we are going is a great help to making choices now on how to respond to current struggles.

How do we live in the tension between what God's people currently are and the unified faith, knowledge, and maturity that God is moving us all toward? Paul has already given instructions on the necessity of humility and persevering love to maintain unity in the Body of Christ. Now, he gives us a concise summary statement we would all do well to make the guiding principle for all of our relationships within and without the church—*speaking the truth in love.*

The first thing I notice in this phrase is that speaking the truth is not necessarily loving in and of itself. I grew up in a segment of Christianity in which the greatest command was minimized while obnoxious methods of proclaiming the truth were promoted. During my teenage years, I asked one pastor why our church never talked about the greatest command to love. His response was that "liberal" churches had abused the concept of love so much that he was justified in rudely proclaiming truth without any effort to be loving and obedient to the greatest command. Paul is teaching here that both positions—love without truth and truth without love—are unhelpful to, and downright destructive of, the ultimate goal that God has painted for us of the mature, unified, doctrinally steady Body of Christ. We must both speak the truth and be loving. The two are not synonymous. We must not choose one or the other, and we must not delude ourselves into thinking that the fact we have one of them right excuses us from incorporating the other. We must do both!

I think of truth as the gas and love as the oil in the engine of Christian community. Without the truth, we are going nowhere. We are powerless, living in a world of relativity with no foundation on which to firmly stand. But without love, friction quickly arises and destroys the working parts of the engine.

When discussing the concept of love, some might argue, "But is it loving to allow someone to continue in their folly? Is it loving to look past sin?" This argument implies that sometimes love might look unloving—that even though the words expressed or actions taken might not LOOK like the description of love in I Corinthians 13, they really were loving because the person who did them held love as their motive. This logic trap seems to justify using words and actions to confront sin that are not characteristic of Biblical love at all.

Fortunately, we are not left with the task of determining what is or is not loving on our own because Paul does not deal with this concept subjectively. We have already mentioned it once, but it bears repeating here. The term love is not used in Scripture the same way it is used in our culture. Biblically, it is not a touchy feely emotion that leaves you warm and fuzzy but is otherwise hard to define. Instead, God gives us clear instructions in I Corinthians 13 as to exactly what he means when he instructs us to speak the truth in love. Did we speak truth kindly, patiently, and humbly? Or were we envious, proud, and boastful? Were we rude, self-seeking, and easily angered? Did we keep a list of the wrongs we suffered? Did we secretly take joy in evil? Or did we rejoice in the truth and protect others? Did we give the benefit of the doubt, believe the best, hope, and endure with others?

With the 1 Corinthians 13 definition of love in mind, it is easy to see that love does not require sin to be overlooked. It requires that our confrontation of sin be consistent with the example of Christ for the unity and growth of the body. Any argument that diminishes the importance of love in how we handle sin is in conflict with Ephesians 4 and I Corinthians 13, placing Biblical unity at risk. By the I Corinthians 13 definition, love is not simply a characteristic we should have when there is no sin, but it defines how we respond when there is sin. In fact, some of I Corinthians 13's characteristics of love **have no function at all except in response to sin and conflict.**

In love

In Ephesians 4:15-16, Paul continues drawing the picture of the finished product that God is making for himself—the mature Body of Christ, with Christ as the Head and individual members joined and held together, growing and working properly together. At the end of this section he repeats the words that are becoming the central idea when we consider what distinguishes healthy church practices from unhealthy ones—*in love*.

It may seem that I am overemphasizing the issue of love. However, since Jesus teaches that loving God and loving our neighbor are the greatest commandments, i. e. the most important things, I think it would be helpful for us to park on the concept of Biblical love for a moment longer and meditate on other Scriptures that teach us about the term.

Love is absolutely essential to Christian testimony. It is the key component of evangelism.

John 13:35 By this all people will know that you are my disciples, if you have love for one another.

In fact, if you do not get Biblical love and exhibit it to others, John goes as far to say in I John 4 that you do not know God at all.

7 Beloved, let us love one another, for love is from God, and whoever loves has been born of God and knows God. 8 Anyone who does not love does not know God, because God is love. 9 In this the love of God was made manifest among us, that God sent his only Son into the world, so that we might live through him…. 19 We love because he first loved us. 20 If anyone says, "I love God," and hates his brother, he is a liar; for he who does not love his brother whom he has seen cannot love God whom he has not seen. 21 And this commandment we have from him: whoever loves God must also love his brother.

There is no perfect church. Perfection right now is a totally unreasonable standard to expect of a church. The Bible is clear that the perfection Christ promises to work in us is not going to be fully realized until we are seated with him in heaven. I Corinthians 13:12 says that we are seeing a dim, distorted reflection in a mirror right now. The clear picture will be seen only when we are face to face with Jesus in heaven.

We are part of an imperfect Church—both corporately and individually. And imperfect churches only demonstrate the profound need for consistent love. Without love, every issue is potentially divisive; but with it, the details can be covered with grace. Consider 1 Peter 4:8, "Above all, love each other deeply, because love covers over a multitude of sins." I love the phrase, "love covers a multitude of sins." The idea is not that love sweeps sin under the carpet. Rather, love keeps others out of the room until the appropriate people can deal with the sin. Love gives us a specific way for speaking the truth, for teaching correct doctrine, for calling others (and ourselves) to repentance, and it involves kindness, gentleness, humility, and patience. You cannot present truth without love and expect a healthy church.

Here are powerful words from Stott.

Thank God there are those in the contemporary church who are determined at all costs to defend and uphold God's revealed truth. But sometimes they are conspicuously lacking in love. When they think they smell heresy, their nose begins to twitch, their muscles ripple, and the light of battle enters their eye. They seem to enjoy nothing more than a fight. Others make the opposite mistake. They are determined at all costs to maintain and exhibit brotherly love, but in order to do so are prepared even to sacrifice the central truths of revelation. Both these tendencies are unbalanced and unbiblical. Truth becomes hard if it is not softened by love; love becomes soft if it is not strengthened by truth. The apostle call us to hold the two together, which should not be difficult for Spirit-filled believers, since the Holy Spirit is himself 'the Spirit of truth' (John 14:17), and his firstfruit is "love" (Galatians 5:22). There is no other route than this to a fully mature Christian unity.[38]

Reflections

_____
_____
_____
_____
_____
_____
_____
_____
_____
_____
_____
_____
_____
_____
_____
_____
_____
_____
_____
_____
_____

[38] Stott, p. 172.

Chapter 17 Ephesians 4: 17-24

17 Now this I say and testify in the Lord, that you must no longer walk as the Gentiles do, in the futility of their minds. 18 They are darkened in their understanding, alienated from the life of God because of the ignorance that is in them, due to their hardness of heart. 19 They have become callous and have given themselves up to sensuality, greedy to practice every kind of impurity. 20 But that is not the way you learned Christ!— 21 assuming that you have heard about him and were taught in him, as the truth is in Jesus, 22 to put off your old self, which belongs to your former manner of life and is corrupt through deceitful desires, 23 and to be renewed in the spirit of your minds, 24 and to put on the new self, created after the likeness of God in true righteousness and holiness.

I love the title Stott gives to the chapter in his book on this section of Scripture. He calls it *A New Set of Clothes*.[39] That is a beautiful picture illustrating the teaching in this section. When God sought and found us, we were miserable, wretched orphans in filthy rags on the street. Then he adopted us into his household with the full benefits of being his beloved child. However, he does not leave us as he found us. He is not content for us to remain in our filth. He transforms us, washes us, and puts on us an entirely new and different way of living, a new set of clothes.

Futility of their minds

Paul begins this section with a detailed look at our old clothes, describing it with the interesting phrase *futility of mind*. The Greek root of the word that is translated *futility* indicates something that is devoid of truth and useless, without purpose, success, or results.[40] It is sometimes translated as vanity. In our former days before we knew Christ, we walked in the futility of our minds. Our thinking was ineffective, powerless, and empty. It was weak and unable to help us. Perhaps you can remember a time in your own life that was characterized by this phrase. You lived trying to work things out in your head, constantly thwarted by your ineffective thought patterns that were powerless to help you figure out how to change your life and bring you happiness.

Verses 18-19 expand on this idea. What do futile thought patterns look like? They are *darkened, alienated, ignorant, hard,* and *calloused*. The result is that people thinking this way are given over to sensual, greedy practices. The Greek word for sensual is interesting. It gives insight into what goes on in a heart held hostage by futile thought patterns. The term means unbridled lust and not only in a sexual sense.[41] They are given over to unrestrained behavior. If they want it, they pursue it. Normal restrictions of law or decency do not bind them. They are given to excess and outrageous shamelessness. Paul finishes the description with the phrase, "greedy to practice every

---

[39] Stott, p. 174.
[40] Strongs, s. v. "Mataios."
[41] Ibid, s. v. "Aselgeia."

kind of impurity." That is a sad, miserable, perverse condition. How hopeless it would be if this section of Ephesians ended here.

But that is not the way you learned Christ

Similar to the opening of chapter 2 of Ephesians, the starkness of the description of our condition apart from Christ makes these next words so beautiful in contrast. This is not what we have learned from Christ! In Christ, we have a completely different example. In Christ, we have a new way of walking—not in the futility of our minds, but in the hope and empowerment of the gospel.

The wording of this phrase is especially noteworthy. It is not that I simply learned about Christ along with other good things but that Christ himself is the sum and substance of all God is teaching us. Christ himself is the catechism. Christ is God's doctrinal statement. Paul goes on to say in verse 21 that the "truth is in Jesus". His use of Jesus instead of Christ is pointing specifically to the life he lived before us on earth.[42] Jesus claims this for himself in John 14:6.

> Jesus said to him, "I am the way, and the truth, and the life. No one comes to the Father except through me.

Paul tells us in Romans 8:29 that "For those whom (God) foreknew he also predestined to be conformed to the image of his Son, in order that he might be the firstborn among many brothers." We learned of foreknowledge and predestination in Ephesians 1. Well, the entire purpose of God's planning for our salvation before time began is realized in this passage. God is transforming us into image bearers of Christ. He is not leaving us the way he found us. He is putting new clothes on us—new natures, new choices, new loves, and a new identity. If you want to know exactly where he is taking us, look at Christ's example. Learn from him.

> John 13:15 For I have given you an example, that you also should do just as I have done to you.

> Matthew 11:29 Take my yoke upon you, and learn from me, for I am gentle and lowly in heart, and you will find rest for your souls.

> 1 Peter 2:21 For to this you have been called, because Christ also suffered for you, leaving you an example, so that you might follow in his steps.

> 1 John 2:6 whoever says he abides in him ought to walk in the same way in which he walked.

One of the most valuable devotional studies I ever did was rereading through the gospels as an adult. Many of us who come from churched backgrounds tend to skip over the gospels. Instead, we attempt "harder" books in our Bible study. I was convicted that I needed to spend time studying the life of Jesus for myself. Despite the fact that I had heard every Bible story in Sunday school growing up, I was constantly amazed at all the details I had missed about his life and

---

[42] Stott, p. 179.

ministry. It clarified so many things for me both within and without Christianity. In Christ, I see by example all that God is changing me to be.

Put off, be renewed, and put on

I have heard many sermons over the years on this section of Ephesians. Most left me feeling like the weight of responsibility for putting away my sins lay on my shoulders alone. It was a good day when I studied these verses in light of the connected, coherent teaching of the whole of Ephesians. Without recognizing the fullness of all we have in Christ and the power at work on our behalf through him according to Ephesians 1 and 2, trying to put off our old self and put on the new self is completely impossible. This passage taken out of context sets up believers for failure.

Paul is talking here specifically about our sanctification—that process by which God changes us from wretched orphans abandoned on the street to the beautiful bride of Christ adorned in righteousness. The Bible is the best commentary on itself, and Ephesians is not the only place it talks about our sanctification. It is helpful to look at other Scripture to give us clarity on how God sanctifies us. Consider 2 Corinthians 3:18.

> And we, who with unveiled faces all reflect the Lord's glory, are being transformed into his likeness with ever-increasing glory, which comes from the Lord, who is the Spirit.

The passive voice here indicates that we are not doing the transforming. Instead, we are being transformed by the Spirit. This is one of the primary functions of the Holy Spirit in the Trinity. The Bible refers to it in 2 Thessalonians 2:13 and 1 Peter 1:2 as the "sanctifying work of the Spirit."

The term passive may raise concerns in some of you reading this. You may think this sounds like we just lay back motionless on the floor while the Spirit does all the work. The Scripture gives us better examples. Consider Moses' actions when Amalek fought Israel in Exodus 20.

> 9 So Moses said to Joshua, "Choose for us men, and go out and fight with Amalek. Tomorrow I will stand on the top of the hill with the staff of God in my hand." 10 So Joshua did as Moses told him, and fought with Amalek, while Moses, Aaron, and Hur went up to the top of the hill. 11 Whenever Moses held up his hand, Israel prevailed, and whenever he lowered his hand, Amalek prevailed. 12 But Moses' hands grew weary, so they took a stone and put it under him, and he sat on it, while Aaron and Hur held up his hands, one on one side, and the other on the other side. So his hands were steady until the going down of the sun. 13 And Joshua overwhelmed Amalek and his people with the sword.

God fought the battle, but Moses participated. Moses' job was to reach out to God, but God was solely responsible for defeating the enemy. While that is a helpful Biblical analogy of our participation with God in the work he does for us, the Bible refers specifically to this joint participation in Leviticus 20 and Philippians 2.

> Leviticus 20:7-8 Consecrate yourselves and be holy, because I am the LORD your God. Keep my decrees and follow them. I am the LORD, who makes you holy.

Philippians 2:12-13 Therefore, my dear friends, as you have always obeyed—not only in my presence, but now much more in my absence—continue to work out your salvation with fear and trembling, for it is God who works in you to will and to act according to his good purpose.

In Leviticus 20, we are commanded to be holy (sanctified or set apart for God's purposes) because God is making us holy. In Philippians 2, we are told to work *out* what God is working *in*. God is working *in* and *with* me, so that I show outwardly what He is changing me to be. Any righteousness we exhibit outwardly is a result of our inner relationship with Christ. We cannot separate the two.

With this foundation in mind, let us go back to Paul's words in this section of Ephesians 4.

22 to put off your old self, which belongs to your former manner of life and is corrupt through deceitful desires, 23 and to be renewed in the spirit of your minds, 24 and to put on the new self, created after the likeness of God in true righteousness and holiness.

While we are passively being transformed (2 Cor. 3:18), we are also proactively putting off our old self and putting on our new self. That new self is entirely wrapped up in the image of God that he created us to be, characterized by the true, authentic, Biblical righteousness and holiness we have learned in Christ.

Interestingly, Paul talks about this same concept in Colossians 3 but uses wording that indicates that the putting off of the old nature and putting on of the new is already completed.

9 Do not lie to one another, seeing that you have put off the old self with its practices 10 and have put on the new self, which is being renewed in knowledge after the image of its creator.

This is becoming what you are. God has broken the chains that enslaved you to sin and given you a new nature. He has put off the old and put on the new at our birth in Christ. Now we are becoming in reality what God has already declared us to be in heaven—fully righteous according to Christ's example. You may be frustrated by the dueling tenses of verbs in these instructions—the tension between divine sovereignty and human responsibility. The Bible definitely asserts both, but the tension fades if we remember Paul's teaching in Ephesians 1. We have an unchanging spiritual reality in the heavenly places guaranteed for us by the deposit of the Holy Spirit. We are becoming on earth what God has already affirmed us to be in heaven. What we have now in Ephesians 4 is God's design for closing the gap between the two, what Francis Schaeffer called "possessing our possessions."

The renewing in Ephesians 4:23 once again reflects a passive voice. We are not doing the renewing. Instead, we are allowing ourselves to be renewed by someone else. This is consistent with all Paul has taught us up to this point. God is doing something new for us and to us through Christ. He is renewing our minds. And we are working in conjunction with him—for apart from him, we can do nothing (John 15:5). It is crucial to understand that our transformation into Christlikeness, putting off the old man and putting on the new, is a joint venture with God in which God does the heavy work. When we struggle with sin, we can cast ourselves fully upon

Christ and expect him to meet us in our struggle and equip us to obey. Apart from such dependence on Christ, we are doomed to failure. As Stott says,

> In all this teaching the divine and the human are beautifully blended. In the command to exchange our old humanity for a new one, Paul is not implying that we can bring about our own new birth. Nobody has ever given birth to himself. The very concept is ludicrous. No, the new humanity we assume is God's creation, not ours. Nevertheless, when God recreates us in Christ according to his own likeness, we entirely concur with what he has done. We 'put off' our old life, turning away from it in distaste, and we 'put on' the new life he has created, embracing it and welcoming it with joy. In a word, recreation (what God does) and repentance (what we do by his grace) belong together and cannot be separated.[43]

I have areas in my life that I hate—places that I repeatedly sin and yearn for lasting change. One issue that I have struggled with a good bit is my weight. On one hand, I struggle with the sin of gluttony. My god is my belly, and I obey it anytime it speaks. On the other hand, I struggle with vanity. I want to be beautiful in the emptiest sense of the term. My old man seems alive and well. How do I battle it and put on a new way of living that reflects all I am in Christ?

For me, the answer is, simply put, the gospel. I have tried a long list of diet and exercise methods. There is always something new to try—some diet that worked like a miracle for someone I know, and, because it worked for him or her, it should also work for me. I then feel pressure to do the same, but instead of feeling motivated, I feel condemned because it never works for me the same way.

But God has called me to himself and is renewing my mind. He has given me an inheritance in Christ that transcends my ability to fully understand. He loves me with a love that surpasses knowledge. And he wants my god to be himself, not my belly. He wants me to live for eternity, not vain beauty. So I wrestle with him—"God, enlighten me to the hope of my calling. Show me how my inheritance in Christ equips me to deal with my sin. Renew my mind so that I may put off both gluttony and vanity and put on new ways of dealing with food, exercise, and body image that are like Christ."

As I wrestled with God, an odd thing happened. I slowly started to lose weight. Let me stop and say that this illustration is not about how to successfully lose weight. This is just an illustration, and I personally think my "success" (if that's what you want to call it) started long before I ever lost a pound. I believe it started the moment I began to wrestle with God on how the gospel applied to this issue. When I began to look to the gospel instead of a diet program, the Lord began renewing my mind in a peaceful, sustaining way that has affected my outlook on much more than just my weight

After years of gluttony and vanity, God renewed my mind on the issue of my weight. He changed my heart so that the lifestyle changes I made were not chores, but pleasures. I can only attribute this to his grace and mercy--to the gospel itself. Without God renewing my mind and enlightening me to my inheritance in him, my attempts at putting off and putting on were powerless.

This is just one small example in my life of how God is transforming me. Where in your life is God moving you to put off old and put on new ways of dealing with issues that reflect Christ's

---

[43] Stott, p. 182.

example? How does your inheritance in him equip you to change? How is he renewing your mind and changing how you think about the issues with which you struggle?

Reflections

_____

_____

_____

_____

_____

_____

_____

_____

_____

_____

_____

_____

_____

_____

_____

_____

_____

_____

_____

_____

_____

_____

_____

_____

_____

_____

_____

_____

Chapter 18 Ephesians 4: 25-29

25 Therefore, having put away falsehood, let each one of you speak the truth with his neighbor, for we are members one of another. 26 Be angry and do not sin; do not let the sun go down on your anger, 27 and give no opportunity to the devil. 28 Let the thief no longer steal, but rather let him labor, doing honest work with his own hands, so that he may have something to share with anyone in need. 29 Let no corrupting talk come out of your mouths, but only such as is good for building up, as fits the occasion, that it may give grace to those who hear.

Give no opportunity to the devil

Now Paul gives us four specific applications to the previous instructions on putting off the old and putting on the new. The old man was characterized by lies and falsehoods. The new man speaks truthfully. The old man sinned in his anger. The new man recognizes his anger and keeps short accounts with others so that his anger does not become an opportunity for Satan to sow seeds of bitterness. The old man took what was not his. The new man not only does not steal, but he shares his possessions with those who have need. The old man spoke in ways that corrupted and tore others down. The new man speaks in the exact opposite way, building up others with timely words that minister grace to the hearer.

I am particularly intrigued by the phrase in verse 27, "and give no opportunity to the devil." At the end of Ephesians, Paul is going to give us strong instructions on holding our ranks against Satan's attacks. Here, he warns against holes in our defenses that give Satan a foothold to use against us. The Greek word translated *opportunity* means power or an occasion for acting.[44] When we are angry with someone and hold on to that anger, we give Satan a powerful open door that invites him to step in and act against us and others. Many great public conflicts between believers started first with unresolved anger in quiet, private places.

The context of these instructions is the unity we are to pursue diligently in the community of Christ. Paul's instructions at the beginning of this chapter were to diligently work to maintain the unity in Christ that the Spirit has already given us. Here, he reminds us again that "we are members one of another" (v. 25). While these instructions are helpful in all of our relationships, they are of utmost importance in our relationships within the Body of Christ.

Surely most of us reading this will feel conviction somewhere in this passage. If your life is still characterized by lying, anger, stealing, or speech that tears others down, how do you move from the old ways of doing things to the new ways you are learning in Christ? I cannot overemphasize our complete dependence on God for this transformation. When most of us struggle with sin, especially ongoing habitual sin, we tend to isolate ourselves from God. Instead, we need to cast

---

[44] Strongs, s. v. "topos."

ourselves on him and take advantage of every privilege we have through our inheritance in Jesus Christ.

Reflections

_____

_____

_____

_____

_____

_____

_____

_____

_____

_____

_____

_____

_____

_____

_____

_____

_____

_____

_____

_____

_____

_____

_____

_____

_____

_____

_____

_____

Chapter 19 Ephesians 4:29-32

29 Let no corrupting talk come out of your mouths, but only such as is good for building up, as fits the occasion, that it may give grace to those who hear. 30 And do not grieve the Holy Spirit of God, by whom you were sealed for the day of redemption. 31 Let all bitterness and wrath and anger and clamor and slander be put away from you, along with all malice. 32 Be kind to one another, tenderhearted, forgiving one another, as God in Christ forgave you.

I am going to include verse 29 again in this section since the thoughts from the previous verses flow right into this one. In terms of putting off the old man and putting on the new, Paul now zooms in on the issue of our language. The amount of time he spends on this one particular issue should raise our awareness to just how important it is. Nothing reflects the profound nature of our change in Christ like our words, and I am not talking about simple cussing or foul language here. That is a minor application of a passage that encompasses so much more. I have known my fair share of Christians who would blush at the mere suggestion of a cuss word but still manage to tear down the Body of Christ with their language in many painful ways. The bottom line is that our words carry significant power for both good and evil in the Body of Christ.

Before we look at Paul's instructions in detail, we ought to note that Scripture says much about our words in both the Old and New Testament.

Ecclesiastes 10:12 (NIV) Words from a wise man's mouth are gracious, but a fool is consumed by his own lips.

Proverbs 11:13 Whoever goes about slandering reveals secrets, but he who is trustworthy in spirit keeps a thing covered.

Proverbs 16:28 A dishonest man spreads strife, and a whisperer separates close friends.

Paul's instructions to the Ephesians reflect God's plan for his children since time began. Our words are to bring grace and restoration. But if you have any experience in the church, you know that the tongue is often the last place in which Christians transform. People may put off lying or sex outside of marriage or drunkenness. But they will hang on to ugly speech that tears others down until it is pried out of their dying hands. Despite the clarity with which Scripture speaks of abusive language, people desire to hang on to their perceived right to speak about others as they see fit. Abusive language is rampant in the church, even among many public Christian leaders. For me, coming to understand the wealth of my sin in this area transformed me in ways that reached far beyond what we traditionally think of as bad language.

Building up and giving grace

Perhaps the best way to handle this section of Ephesians is to focus on what God planned our speech to be, not all the ways we corrupt it. What does speech among those who are conformed to Christ's image look like? According to verse 29 our talk should be good and useful for *building up as fits the occasion.* In so doing, it will then *give grace to those who hear.* What a great summary statement of God's plan for our language.

First, it builds up others. It does not tear someone down. It enlightens them, strengthens them, encourages them, and so forth. It points them positively in the direction of Christ. This is the opposite of taking someone down a notch or proving our point at another's expense. Second, this talk fits the occasion. Ecclesiastes 3 says that there is "a time to weep and a time to laugh, a time to mourn and a time to dance, ... a time to be silent and a time to speak." (v. 4, 7) When we speak to our brothers and sisters in Christ, we need to know what time it is. We need to seek the Spirit's timing and not our own, speaking with words that fit the needs of that particular moment, not the agenda that we have had in the back of our head for a month. I cannot tell you how many times I have missed the mark here, especially in my marriage.

The third part of this is that language that reflects Christ *give(s) grace to those who hear.* This is one of the most inspiring thoughts to me in this entire section of Ephesians. I love how the old King James words this, "that it may minister grace unto the hearers." I am humbled and awed to think that my words could be a conduit of God's grace to someone in need. That is the kind of speech for which I long to both hear from others and speak myself. You know when you are in the presence of this person. They speak, the Spirit meets you in their words, and you sense God's grace to you. You may think, "Well, they just have a gracious personality. I could never speak that way." But that is not true! Gracious speech in the gospel sense of the term is not caused by someone's personality. This is God's image bursting forth in this person. You too are being conformed to the image of Christ and called to a pattern of speech through which God's grace flows and ministers life to the hearer. If that seems like a far off goal well out of your reach, be encouraged, dear sister! This is exactly the direction in which God is leading you. Your spiritual inheritance in Christ is certain. God is transforming you slowly but surely in Christ's image. Yield to him, and you will see the new man emerge over time through the renewed mind that God is working in you.

Do not grieve the Holy Spirit

The Greek word for *grieve* in Ephesians 4:30 is also used in Matthew 26 to describe Jesus' state in the Garden of Gethsemane right before his execution.[45]

37 And taking with him Peter and the two sons of Zebedee, he began to be *sorrowful* and troubled. 38 Then he said to them, "My soul is very sorrowful, even to death; remain here, and watch with me." 39 And going a little farther he fell on his face and prayed, saying, "My Father, if it be possible, let this cup pass from me; nevertheless, not as I will, but as you will."

---

[45] Strongs, s. v. "lupeo."

90

Jesus was sorrowful and troubled. His heart was weighed down. It is sobering to associate such words with the mental state of our Savior. Sometimes it is easier to think of God as emotionally detached from the details of our lives. But Scripture presents God the Father, Son, and Spirit as connected with us emotionally. We are not merely practicing a religion. These Scriptures remind us we are in an intimate relationship with our God who is sometimes grieved, sorrowful, and distressed in his relationship with us.

Paul's words here remind me of 2 Thessalonians 5:19, "Do not quench the Spirit." Specifically, this verse in Ephesians on grieving the Spirit is right in the middle of a talk on the power of our words. The context in which we are grieving the Spirit is language that tears down rather than builds up, that sucks grace out of the room rather than being the conduit through which grace is applied. Though there are many indicators of a life not filled by the Spirit, our tolerance of speech in our homes, churches, marriages, and friendships that tears down rather than builds up is a definite starting point. Such language grieves the Spirit and quenches his work.

Paul says as well that it is this Spirit "by whom you were sealed for the day of redemption." Since the context of this passage is still the unity of the Body and our need to diligently work to preserve it, it makes sense why the dissension caused by our words would certainly grieve the Spirit who has sealed us together in Christ.

I have had the most practice in this concept through conflict in my marriage. I have often resorted to nagging, manipulative speech in my home, and that kind of talk has never once contributed to gospel-centered reconciliation with my husband. Instead, it grieves and quenches the Spirit. It makes reconciliation less of a possibility, not more. But when I tap into the wealth of my inheritance in Christ and the power of the resurrection at work on my behalf, then I can begin to speak words that fit the needs of the moment and minister grace to the hearer. That is when reconciliation starts to become possible through the Spirit's conviction.

Reflections

_____

_____

_____

_____

_____

_____

_____

_____

_____

_____

_____

Chapter 20 Ephesians 4: 31-32

31 Let all bitterness and wrath and anger and clamor and slander be put away from you, along with all malice. 32 Be kind to one another, tenderhearted, forgiving one another, as God in Christ forgave you.

Tenderhearted

We are called to put away bitterness (conversation marked by resentment, cynicism, antagonism, or ill-will), anger, clamor (heated expressions of discontent or frustration), slander (abusive attacks on a person's character or good name), and malice (ill will toward another that includes a desire to injure them emotionally or physically). In place of it, we are commanded to be kind, tenderhearted, and forgiving JUST AS CHRIST FORGAVE US.   In a minute, we will park on the last phrase of this chapter. But for a moment, I want to focus on the term *tenderhearted*.

The Greek word translated *tenderhearted* is used just one other time in the New Testament, in which Peter sums up Paul's instructions in Ephesians 4 pretty well.

I Peter 3:8 Finally, all of you, have unity of mind, sympathy, brotherly love, a tender heart, and a humble mind.

A tender heart. This is in contrast to a hard heart. A tender heart is easily moved by someone else's suffering or sorrow. The Greek word can also be translated compassionate.[46] Thanks to my eighth grade Latin teacher, I know that the term compassion is from the root Latin words for suffering together (com—with or together, and pati—to suffer). I see also in Scripture that compassion is one of God's attributes. God is known for his tenderness toward and compassion for his children.

Exodus 34:6 (NIV) And he passed in front of Moses, proclaiming, "The LORD, the LORD, the compassionate and gracious God, slow to anger, abounding in love and faithfulness.

Meditating on the root of the term compassion opened my eyes to something about my Father. He does not just generally feel sorry for me or love me with a standoffish type of concern. He enters into my suffering. He suffers WITH me. One of the clearest illustrations of this in the life of Jesus is his interaction with Mary and Martha at the death of Lazarus in John 11.

32 Now when Mary came to where Jesus was and saw him, she fell at his feet, saying to him, "Lord, if you had been here, my brother would not have died." 33 When Jesus saw her weeping, and the Jews

---

[46] Strongs, s. v. "eusplagchnos."

who had come with her also weeping, he was deeply moved in his spirit and greatly troubled. 34 And he said, "Where have you laid him?" They said to him, "Lord, come and see." 35 Jesus wept.

Jesus has already told the disciples that he is going to bring Lazarus back to life, so he is not weeping for Lazarus. He knows he is going to heal him and teach Mary and Martha something precious about himself as God. Yet, he still enters into their pain at their brother's death and weeps with them. Though knowing very well the good outcome coming soon (Lazarus' complete healing), he was moved and troubled by their sorrow. He had compassion on them. God is calling on you and I to do the same to others. We are to be soft-hearted toward them, willing to enter into their sorrow.

Forgiving one another as Christ has forgiven you

Once again, it is the gospel—the forgiveness we have in Christ through his death on the cross and all the corresponding benefits that go with it—that equips us to live out these instructions. Years ago, I came across a poem whose source is unknown and wrote it in my journal.

> You are writing a Gospel
> A chapter each day,
> By the deeds that you do
> And the words that you say.
> Men read what you write,
> Whether faithful or true:
> Just what is the Gospel
> According to you?

What is the true gospel? In contrast, what is the gospel that my life and words articulate to others? Just what is the gospel according to me? The New Testament repeatedly teaches that grace, humility, love and forgiveness are the essential aspects of a life that accurately understands the gospel for itself and lives it out for others (John 13:35, I John 3:10, Luke 6:35). God teaches clearly that those who are unable to forgive others have completely missed the heart of the gospel to themselves.

The Greek word for forgive in Ephesians 4:32 is *charizomai*. Its definition is a bit broader than what I traditionally think of as forgiveness. It means to do a favor for, be gracious toward, give graciously to, pardon, freely bestow on another, or restore one to another.[47] It is derived from *charis*, the Greek word for grace, which we talked about in depth in Section 1. I will not rehash all we said in that section, but I will repeat the key thoughts here. When you give back what is earned, expected, or deserved, it is not *charis*—it is not grace. Instead, you are just doing what seems reasonable to you. In contrast, grace is an unreasonably good response that does what is unexpected and undeserved. When we give grace to the undeserving, we give evidence to our relationship with our Father in heaven, for he is good to those who do not deserve it. He is full of grace.

---

[47] Strongs, s. v. "charizomai."

As for forgiveness, consider how Jesus uses the term *charizomai* in Luke 7.

42 When they could not pay, he *cancelled the debt* of both. Now which of them will love him more?" 43 Simon answered, "The one, I suppose, for whom he *cancelled the* larger *debt*." And he said to him, "You have judged rightly."

God has forgiven us. He has cancelled our debt against him because Christ has paid the full price for our sins. We know from Ephesians 1 that, not only has he cancelled our debt, he has also lavished on us a great inheritance in him. We owe no debt to him and now in fact have a great surplus in his coffers. The kicker is that he tells us that we must do the same. I used to think that it was one think to be forgiven, but another entirely to forgive the one who has hurt me. But I am growing in my understanding that the two are inextricably intertwined.

Several passages in the New Testament teach us to forgive others SO THAT God may forgive us.

Mark 11:25 And whenever you stand praying, forgive, if you have anything against anyone, so that your Father also who is in heaven may forgive you your trespasses."

Other passages in the New Testament, along with Ephesians 4:32, teach that we must now forgive others because God has ALREADY forgiven us.

Colossians 3:13 bearing with one another and, if one has a complaint against another, forgiving each other; as the Lord has forgiven you, so you also must forgive.

This dual way of speaking of the order of forgiveness indicates to me that my response to others' sins against me is the great barometer for gauging my own understanding of the gospel for myself. If you are struggling with extending grace and forgiveness to someone else, preach the gospel to yourself even as you cancel the debt of the one who owes you. We most often struggle with forgiving the debts of others against us because we have not fully understood the extent of both our debts against God and the finality of his forgiveness of us.

The path of forgiveness and healing can seem deep and complicated. How many years have some of us spent in therapy processing the abuse we have experienced at the hands of others? But the gospel seems to demystify and uncomplicate it. There is something about God's instructions on reconciliation and forgiveness that are straightforward. Forgive. Cancel the debt. Extend the pardon. Let go of your rights. Release the one who has sinned against you from all they owe you in reparation.*

Forgiveness is not fair. That's the entire point. It is *charizomai* because you have the right to extract heavy repayment. God's call is to let go of that right. Our response does not have to be self defense in proportion to the harm done to us or harboring of resentment until reparation is made. There is a better way. It does not make sense and seems counterintuitive. But actually

---

* Please do not read this as dismissive of Christian counseling. A counselor who walks with a wounded believer as long as it takes is an invaluable resource. However, though getting there may be complicated, the end goal of gospel forgiveness is a straightforward concept.

letting go of our rights to reparation and canceling the debt against us does more than just let the other person off the hook. It actually is key to our own healing.

We have reached the end of Ephesians 4, which began with a call to eagerly and diligently work to preserve the unity of the Body of Christ that the Spirit has created in us. Paul has given us numerous practical instructions to accomplish that objective, all centered around the idea of humble, longsuffering love for one another. He ends the exhortation to preserve unity with the call to forgive others as God has forgiven us. Jesus gave everything he had to create this unity. He emptied himself of his rights and took on the form of a servant, even humbling himself to die on the cross (Philippians 2). The progression of this chapter reflects that we are called to love the Body and sacrifice ourselves just as Christ has done. We are called to do no more and no less than simply follow his example on how to handle discord and conflict in the Church.

Reflections

_____

_____

_____

_____

_____

_____

_____

_____

_____

_____

_____

_____

_____

_____

_____

_____

_____

_____

_____

_____

Chapter 21 Ephesians 5: 1-2

1 Therefore be imitators of God, as beloved children. 2 And walk in love, as Christ loved us and gave himself up for us, a fragrant offering and sacrifice to God.

No one can accuse Paul of underemphasizing his main points in Ephesians. Perhaps it seems redundant to you. Instead, it reminds me of a slow, deep soaking rain. As Paul builds his ideas, he keeps emphasizing the foundation. The first time he said it, I noted it. The second time he said it, it sank in a little deeper. The third time, I started to understand how profound these ideas were. The fourth, fifth, and sixth times … well, it is now settling deep into my psyche. God has created me to reflect his image and that means loving others the way Christ loves me. Forgive the redundancy of this next section, but since Paul saw fit to repeat these ideas, I feel that I would not do justice to the book if I did not do the same.

Therefore imitate God

Once again, Paul is drawing a direct correlation between what he just finished saying in Ephesians 4 and what he is emphasizing again in Ephesians 5. He ended Ephesians 4 with a call for kindness, compassion, and forgiveness to one another in the Body of Christ, even as God in Christ has forgiven us. Now he repeats the call to be like Christ. We are to be imitators of God. This reminds me of the account of God's creation of mankind in Genesis 1.

26 Then God said, "Let us make man in our image, after our likeness. And let them have dominion over the fish of the sea and over the birds of the heavens and over the livestock and over all the earth and over every creeping thing that creeps on the earth."
27 So God created man in his own image,
   in the image of God he created him;
male and female he created them.

God created us, male and female, in his image. In perfection, God's plan was that we would be like him. You might ask, "Like him in what way?" My answer is that we would be like him in every way that makes him unique, set apart, and holy. He created us that his loves and priorities would be our loves and priorities. He created us that his value system would be our value system. He made us to reflect (to shine a mirror back on) all the things that make him who he is.

Adam's sin destroyed much and has resulted in the perversion of the things that God originally created for his good purposes, but now in Christ, we see that God is redeeming all that was lost in the fall. He has made a way for us to once again imitate him and reflect his image. The summary of all of his instructions in Scripture is simply to be imitators of him.

Here is the great intensifier of the summary phrase *be imitators of him*. Walk in love! This reflects directly on the greatest command to love God and love our neighbor repeated in Deuteronomy, Matthew, Mark, and Luke. Here it is from Mark 12.

28 And one of the scribes came up and heard them disputing with one another, and seeing that he answered them well, asked him, "Which commandment is the most important of all?" 29 Jesus answered, "The most important is, 'Hear, O Israel: The Lord our God, the Lord is one. 30 And you shall love the Lord your God with all your heart and with all your soul and with all your mind and with all your strength.' 31 The second is this: 'You shall love your neighbor as yourself.' There is no other commandment greater than these."

Do not miss it, and do not minimize it. God's great calling is to be like him, and this means that we walk in love. Period. That is the great summary of the entire Christian calling. As Jesus says in Mark, "There is no other commandment greater than these."

Recall once again the I Corinthians 13 definition of Biblical love. It gives us concrete ideas of all that he is practically calling us to work out in our own lives. Who is it that God is calling you to sacrificially love in the image of Christ? How is he transforming you and equipping you to love the unlovely? How is he working his image in you so that you can walk humbly and graciously in your interactions with the ungrateful and evil? How does Christ's fragrant offering to God for you change how you view his call on you to love those hard to love as he does?

Reflections

_____
_____
_____
_____
_____
_____
_____
_____
_____
_____
_____
_____
_____
_____
_____
_____

Chapter 22 Ephesians 5: 3-4

3 But sexual immorality and all impurity or covetousness must not even be named among you, as is proper among saints. 4 Let there be no filthiness nor foolish talk nor crude joking, which are out of place, but instead let there be thanksgiving.

Filthiness v. thanksgiving

As I studied this section of Ephesians, it dawned on me that I could write an entire separate manuscript to women just on these two verses.   There is much to unpack here, so I appreciate Stott's summary phrase for these two verses, "Don't joke about sex, but rather give thanks for it."[48] It is helpful to have this overview in mind as we look at the specific parts of these verses. Some reading this might nod their head vehemently in agreement and be content to move on quickly. But I was hit in the gut that this was not going to be a simple, short section on which to write. This is about the redemption of our views of sex—about moving from the sexual perversions brought on by our depravity and replacing it with a view of sex that does not just endure it but actually enjoys God's design and is thankful for it.

On this subject more than any other, I am glad this book is geared toward women and not because I would be embarrassed to write on this subject if it was geared toward men. That is another issue altogether. No, I am overjoyed to write on this to women primarily because *others rarely do.*

Over the years, I have seen more and more written in evangelical circles toward men concerning sexual sin. While I think that is a helpful development, I have realized in terms of sexual sin that women (at least in my culture) have definitely reached equality with men.   Why would churches spend so much time on men's sexual addictions without realizing the need to have a similar focus for women? Perhaps the reason is, that as shameful as it is for a man to struggle with pornography, multiple partners, or the like, the shame our Christian society projects on a woman for such sin is, in my opinion, much worse. Because of the shame attached to sin in this area, Christian women tend to struggle in silence with sexual sin more than any other sin issue in my experience.   Several godly friends of mine, all leaders in women's ministry in their respective churches, shared with me their own experience, calling my attention to the fact that women can struggle with sexual sin as deeply as men. This required them to publicly share their past struggles with sexual sin and was a hard, humbling step for these women to take. But once they were honest with their struggle, other women started coming forward in droves. If you are struggling with

---

[48] Stott, p. 191.

sexual sin, I hope you know that you are not alone and that God is powerful to redeem and restore you.

I am burdened for both those who have struggled with sexual sin and those who have not. In Christian circles, many remnants of the story line from *The Scarlet Letter*—shaming of those who have sinned, self-flagellation by offenders in an attempt to clean their conscience, isolation from Christian community, and so forth—remain the default response to sexual sin. Ephesians equips those of us who have struggled with sexual sin to deal with our sin in Christ and those of us who have not to humbly walk beside those who have without casting shame. If you get anything of the gospel that Paul has presented to this point, you know that sexual sin or not, all of us have sinned against God in dark, alienating ways. But instead of shaming us, God sent his Son to bear the shame for us, and by his wounds we are healed.

In terms of sex, I want to focus on what God is moving us away from, what he is moving us toward, and how he accomplishes this in our lives. First, we see that our old clothing included sexual immorality, all types of impurity, filthiness, foolish talk, and crude joking. We will plod through the definitions of each so that we let Scripture filter out our cultural assumptions and fully understand what God means with these terms.

The Greek term for sexual immorality, *porneia*, covers a wide spectrum—adultery, homosexuality, sex with animals, and general fornication (sex with anyone outside of marriage).[49] The term for all impurity in 5:3 is the same word used in Ephesians 4:19.

> [19]They have become callous and have given themselves up to sensuality, greedy to practice every kind of impurity.

It simply means not pure. To get a better frame of reference for what impurity indicates here, we need to understand what pure, untainted, pollution free sex looks like. What did God intend sex to be? He designed sex to be enjoyed between a husband and a wife. It is not to be sacrificially endured at the expense of one spouse. Nor is it to be pursued for individual selfish enjoyment (I Corinthians 7). Understanding God's good plan for sex allows us to recognize those views of sex that fall short of his standard and fit the very broad category of all impurity.

In both Ephesians 4:19 and 5:13, Paul gives an interesting qualifier with the term *pleonexia* that helps us recognize what things are incompatible with God's pure, untainted plan for sex. In Ephesians 4:19 it is translated greedy, and here it is covetousness.[50] It points to an insatiable desire for more. This unquenchable desire, which even when it gets what it thinks it wants is still not satisfied, is the root of what separates God's good design for sex in marriage with all perversions of it.

Paul then mentions filthiness, foolish talk, and crude joking. The term for filthiness points to something that is dishonorable and is derived from the word translated shameful in verse 12, which we will get to in a bit.[51] Foolish talk is the Greek word *morologia*, which basically means the language of morons or the talk of fools.[52] Finally there is crude joking. The Greek word means

---

[49] Strongs, s. v. "porneia."
[50] Ibid, s. v. "pleonexias"
[51] Ibid, s. v. "aischrotes."
[52] Ibid, s. v. "morologia."

humorous banter. The King James Version uses the simple word "jesting" and is probably the closest translation. Other versions have added the adjective coarse or crude because the instruction against this humorous banter is in the context of sexual impurity.

Some people will adamantly argue that these Greek words have very specific meanings on which we should all agree in our current generation. In my experience, that is a simplistic understanding of both the teaching in this section and our culture in general. I have lived in South Carolina, South Korea, and Seattle, Washington. When I lived in South Carolina, I attached to this instruction a set of words, phrases, and topics that were off limits. Then I moved to South Korea and realized how many of my southern cultural assumptions were irrelevant or outright offensive in this strange new culture I was learning. I learned that some elements of my polite southern behavior actually communicated the exact opposite of what I intended. Then I moved to Seattle and was faced with learning even more about my inadequate understanding of the language of morons and jokes that do not fit the occasion. Not long after I moved to Seattle, I asked a friend who was raised there what she thought of as offensive joking. Her response convicted me of many things about which I had not given much thought.

Each of these Greek terms is rather broad in its definition. Therefore, I find the clarifying phrase, "which are out of place" quite helpful. How do you determine what types of talking and joking are foolish and immoral? Well, they are out of place, they do not meet the needs of the moment, and they do not minister grace to the hearer. This requires us to move beyond checklists of inappropriate words, phrases, or jokes. We have to actually engage with others to be aware of their needs. What type of words fit this occasion? What type of joking (if any) is appropriate in this particular setting with these particular people? What will cause offense? What words or jokes reflect a depraved view of sex? Do my words reflect a fool's view of sex or thanksgiving for sex as God designed it?

This is what God is moving us away from. And we know what he is moving us toward in terms of sex—giving, enjoyable sex between husband and wife as God intended when he created us in perfection in his image. How do we get there? The final phrase from verse 4 is the missing link, "instead let there be thanksgiving." If you are like me, you likely wonder what thanksgiving has to do with the topic at hand. We are moving from self-centered to God-centered views and practices of sex. We are moving away from greedy personal practices to thanksgiving to God in earnest appreciation of all he created it to be. Stott says this well.

> In itself thanksgiving is not an obvious substitute for vulgarity, since the latter is essentially self-centered and the former God-centered. But perhaps this the point that Paul is making …. Paul is setting vulgarity and thanksgiving even more plainly in opposition to each other, namely as alternative pagan and Christian attitudes to sex. Of course Christians have a bad reputation for being negative towards sex. … But the reason why Christians should dislike and avoid vulgarity is not because we have a warped view of sex, and are either ashamed or afraid of it, but because we have a high and holy view of it as being in its right place God's good gift, which we do not want to see cheapened. All God's gifts, including sex, are subjects for thanksgiving, rather than for joking.[53]

---

[53] Stott, p. 192-193.

Reflections

Chapter 23 Ephesians 5:3-4 continued

As I said in the last chapter, I believe that sexual sin is an area in which many Christian women struggle in silence. If you do not struggle with it personally, be thankful, but also recognize that you likely have a close friend who does, albeit in silence and shame. From the soft-core porn of romance novels to hard-core online websites and videos, there is a wide breadth of opportunity for women to participate in sexual sin, with or without a partner. Even though I spent time in the last chapter defining the terms that Paul is using, I do not think I need to focus attention on convicting you or others of their sexual sin. Instead, I think many women are well convicted already and are stuck in the cycle of shame and guilt, hiding their past in great fear of being found out for their sexual history. I am going to take time in this chapter to apply the whole of what we have learned in Ephesians up to this point to the specific area of sexual sin and addiction.

There are many diverse ways we can be sexually immoral, but I want now to focus on the overarching sin that feeds sexual addictions. Understanding the foundation of such sin is our hope for dealing with it successfully for the long term. The foundational sin to which I am referring is the sin of idolatry.

Colossians 3:5 Put to death therefore what is earthly in you: sexual immorality, impurity, passion, evil desire, and covetousness, which is idolatry.

We discussed in the last chapter how Paul links sexual sin to covetousness. He does the same in Colossians 3, adding the additional qualifier of idolatry. The sin of idolatry is clearly seen when you analyze trends among those who successfully conquer one addiction only to move on to another. I caught an episode on a television show that included interviews with several women who had surgery to reduce their stomach size to help them deal with severe obesity. Though each lost significant weight, the point of the show was that they all moved on to excessive behavior in another realm. One became a compulsive shopper, another a gambling addict, and so forth. Some studies indicate that upwards of 30 percent of compulsive eaters that have stomach stapling or lap band surgery transfer their addictions to some other substance.[54]

For believers struggling with sexual sin and addiction, the same transference of addiction can happen. Several friends of mine have told me of overcoming sexual addiction only to realize brand new struggles with gluttony, compulsive shopping, or perfectionism. Their sexual sin was a symptom of something deeper going on in their hearts. They may have managed to stop particularly shameful sexual behavior, but they replaced it with something that, while perhaps more respectable, was still equally controlling of them in place of God.

---

[54] "Suddenly Skinny." The Oprah Winfrey Show. Chicago, Ill. 24 Oct. 2006.

The true condition of their heart was that they simply were not satisfied in God. They did not understand the wealth of their inheritance in him or the power at work on their behalf. They were not so thirsty for him that the inferior satisfaction of other things lost their attraction to them. When they had a longing in their heart, they turned to food, shopping, obsessive compulsive cleaning, pornography, romance novels, or you name it. When we turn to these other things, they become addictive because they cannot satisfy long term. You can drink a gallon but only get a teaspoon of gratification. So you do it more and more trying to pursue that fleeting moment of satisfaction, rest, or peace.

What do you do if you feel stuck in the cycle of sin, shame, and guilt? First, examine yourself, for we often confuse *worldly* sorrow, which only leads to death, with *godly* sorrow over our sins, which leads to repentance.

> 2 Corinthians 7:10 For godly grief produces a repentance that leads to salvation without regret, whereas worldly grief produces death.

How do we recognize the difference between godly and worldly grief over our failings? Worldly sorrow is characterized by feelings of shame and pain that you got caught or hopelessness over ever being cleansed from your sin, and it is only relieved by someone else doing something for you or you doing something for yourself (someone affirming you, someone or something distracting you, you manipulating how others think of you, etc.). In contrast, godly sorrow is sorrow that directs you to Christ. You do not need someone else to do something for you. You do not need to do something for yourself. Instead, you fall flat on your face before God alone, for godly sorrow points you directly to him. Godly sorrow is relieved by faith in what Christ has already done for you.

Many of us spend years of our lives mistaking worldly sorrow on a wide range of sin issues for authentic repentance and then wonder why we never change. **Feeling bad about what you have done is not the same as a godly sorrow that leads to repentance.** This is an important place to examine ourselves. I encourage you to go back to Paul's prayer at the end of Ephesians 1 and personalize it for yourself. "God, open my eyes that I may know you better. Enlighten me to all you have accomplished for me on the cross and the sustaining hope I can have in Christ. I need to understand my inheritance in you. Help me make use of the awesome power of the resurrection at work in me because my sin seems so powerful over me."

God has poured his wrath out on Christ in your place. Instead of wrath, God offers you forgiveness and cleansing through Jesus. We are washed in Jesus' blood. Washed. Cleansed. Purified. Think what it means when you wash away the grime after a day of hard exercise or work. God has scrubbed us in Christ's blood and washed our sin and stain away. Just as the dirt pours off us and flows down the drain never to be seen again, God has washed away our sin and guilt. We smell clean and look clean because WE ARE CLEAN.

> 1 Corinthians 6:11 And such were some of you. But you were washed, you were sanctified, you were justified in the name of the Lord Jesus Christ and by the Spirit of our God.

The journey from sin to restoration is a deeply personal walk that begins with an intimate relationship with Jesus. We know him. We cry out to him. He meets us in our need with forgiveness through his death on the cross. Then we journey with him through this process. Eventually, this walk of repentance and restoration includes confession and reconciliation to those we have wronged.

As previously discussed, habitual sexual sin is evidence of a deeper heart issue—idolatry. Understanding the idols of our heart and the false gods that we worship is rarely an instantaneous process. It takes time in the Word and prayer, asking God to reveal to us the things we allow to stand in the place of God in our hearts. In Colossians 1-3, Paul gives us a long, beautiful discourse on how to deal with our sin that mirrors much of what he is teaching in Ephesians. The bottom line is that we must hold fast to the Head (Jesus Christ). Rules to guard us from sin are minimally helpful at best and often instead rivet our attention toward the sin. **The best guardrail against falling into old sin habits is to be so distracted by the beauty and goodness of Jesus that we lose our taste for the old ways.**

In Colossians 3:2, Paul writes that we must "set [our] minds on things that are above, not on things that are on earth." All of our hope for change is wrapped up in this concept. We have a new passion and, therefore, a new focus. When our minds are focused on our eternal reality in heaven and our spiritual reality in Christ on earth, we are then ready to do effective battle with Satan. All of this stems from a real relationship with Jesus. We do not talk about him. We talk with him. We do not simply listen to what others have to say about the Bible. We read his Word for ourselves. We do not try to fit in with Christian culture. We wrestle with Jesus personally over the hard things in life.

In my own life, I returned again and again to sin that I hated. I hated what I did, and I hated myself for doing it. At times I tried to justify it. Other times I tried to disengage my mind from it altogether and pretend that it did not exist. When such sin goes on and on in our lives, our tendency is to isolate ourselves from God. God hates sin, right?! But that was a self-fulfilling prophecy. When I isolate myself from God because of my sin and shame, I can be assured I will never break the bonds of that sin.

Instead, I had to cast myself on God. "God I am enslaved to something other than you. I cannot free myself on my own. Change me! Change my heart. Change my loves. Open my eyes to all you have bought for me on the cross." And I had to do it again and again. Even when I was profoundly disturbed that I had sinned yet again, I had to cast myself at his feet, call on his mercy, and claim as my own all he has declared me to be in Christ. Over time, God began to take the place of my idols in my heart's affection. A deep conviction that only he could satisfy me started to seep down into my being. I became so enamored by him that those things that use to suck me into the vortex of sin became less and less desirable.

Sister in Christ who struggles with her sexual history, enter God's throne room now by the blood of Jesus Christ and look to him to wash you clean.

Reflections

Chapter 24 Ephesians 5: 5-8

5 For you may be sure of this, that everyone who is sexually immoral or impure, or who is covetous (that is, an idolater), has no inheritance in the kingdom of Christ and God. 6 Let no one deceive you with empty words, for because of these things the wrath of God comes upon the sons of disobedience. 7 Therefore do not become partners with them; 8 for at one time you were darkness, but now you are light in the Lord...

No inheritance

This is the fourth time in Ephesians that Paul has painted the grim, desperate picture of our absolute hopelessness left to ourselves. The first was in the opening of chapter 2, the second in chapter 3, and the third in the middle of chapter 4. This time in chapter 5, he specifically points out the hopelessness of the sexually greedy, who worship a god other than the one true God. They are idolaters and have no inheritance in the kingdom of God. God's wrath is upon them.

Paul is repeating themes of the early chapters of Ephesians. He spoke clearly in chapter 1 of our inheritance in Christ and even prayed specifically at the end of the chapter that we would understand the riches of this inheritance. So his use of the term inheritance here is not pulled out of thin air. The sexually greedy have none of this inheritance in God's kingdom. As much as I want to bask in the beauty of all Paul described of my inheritance in Christ from earlier chapters, he is intent that I understand it in contrast with what I deserve and many will receive—God's wrath and judgment. I would prefer not to have to deal with judgment and the consequences of sin. I would rather meditate on the concepts of grace, love, and mercy without thinking about the other. But I am reminded again and again that the Biblical concepts of grace, love, and mercy completely lose their meaning when removed from the context of God's pending judgment. It is mercy because we deserved wrath. If you downplay God's wrath, you no longer have mercy. You just have general kindness. God would have nothing to overcome. If there was no obstacle in the way, then giving us his good gifts and an eternal inheritance in his kingdom is easy and natural. His mercy is irrelevant without a proper understanding of his judgment.

You were darkness but now are light

Just as Paul did in Ephesians 2, 3 and 4, he does not leave us to despair over our hopeless condition without God. He emphasizes once again that we are not those people anymore. He does not just say that we once walked IN the darkness but now walk IN the light, though the New Testament uses that terminology elsewhere. Here he emphasizes that our entire nature has been changed. We were not IN the darkness—we were the darkness. And now we do not just walk in the light, we ARE the light. He includes the great qualifying phrase *in the Lord* at the end to make sure we do not forget what has made this possible. This is a beautiful picture of the radical transformation we have in Christ.

Paul's words in I Corinthians 6 go right along with his teaching here.

9 Or do you not know that the unrighteous will not inherit the kingdom of God? Do not be deceived: neither the sexually immoral, nor idolaters, nor adulterers, nor men who practice homosexuality, 10 nor thieves, nor the greedy, nor drunkards, nor revilers, nor swindlers will inherit the kingdom of God. 11 And such were some of you. But you were washed, you were sanctified, you were justified in the name of the Lord Jesus Christ and by the Spirit of our God.

I love verse 11—"and such were some of you." We must never forget what we were, but we must also never meditate on our history apart from the beautiful cleansing we now have in Jesus.

Reflections

_____
_____
_____
_____
_____
_____
_____
_____
_____
_____
_____
_____
_____
_____
_____
_____
_____
_____
_____

Chapter 25 Ephesians 5: 8-14

… Walk as children of light 9 (for the fruit of light is found in all that is good and right and true), 10 and try to discern what is pleasing to the Lord. 11 Take no part in the unfruitful works of darkness, but instead expose them. 12 For it is shameful even to speak of the things that they do in secret. 13 But when anything is exposed by the light, it becomes visible, 14 for anything that becomes visible is light. Therefore it says,

"Awake, O sleeper,
and arise from the dead,
and Christ will shine on you."

Walk as children of light

Our earthly reality is that we are waiting (and striving) for our bodies on earth to catch up with our heavenly reality. Paul's instruction to walk as children of light makes sense here. He has already declared us to be light. Now he emphasizes again that we must become what we are. We are to walk like we actually belong in the light. What is the fruit of the light? It is found in all that is good, right, and true.

The concepts of good, right, and true are objective facts in Scripture. Yet, if you introduce those words in conversation, it does not take long to see that people can use them any way that is comfortable. Our job is to figure out what is pleasing to God. Paul uses the word *discern* here, which means to test, examine, or prove in order to determine if something is genuine or not.[55] As children of the light, we are to apply ourselves to examining what is genuinely good, right, and true as God defines the terms. We test and scrutinize according to God's standards, with Jesus Christ as our example. As Paul said earlier, the truth is in Jesus. Christ is the sum and substance of all that is good, right, and true.

Instead expose them

A few years ago, the elders' wives at the church I attended planned a women's retreat entitled "Exposed," taken from this verse in Ephesians. I was a women's ministry leader at the time, but to be honest, I dreaded going to this retreat. The title did not in any way naturally draw me. Personally, I did not want to be exposed and did not care to be a part of something that had set that as its agenda.

---

[55] Strongs, s. v. "dokimazo."

Then I went to the retreat. Each woman that spoke gave brutally honest testimony of where she had been in her darkness, how God had brought her from darkness to light, and all the ways God was still meeting her in her failures. Each one was exposing themselves, bringing their ugly pasts and some of their ugly present into the light. It ended up being one of the most powerful retreats with long lasting outcomes I have ever witnessed. As each speaker spoke on God's redemption of her particular sin (gluttony, sexual addiction, vanity, and so forth), women started understanding that hiding their sin, shame, and guilt was not the answer. Woman after woman started admitting her sin, exposing herself by walking out of the darkness and into the light. While that can be terrifying and cruelly damaging in the wrong context, in the light of the gospel, it was beautiful, redemptive, and uplifting.

When Paul says to take no part in the unfruitful works of darkness and instead expose them, we probably all think of an instance of someone maliciously revealing someone else's sin or shame. When people in darkness rip at others in darkness, there is no good that can come from it. Exposure of sin apart from the gospel is cruel, leaving devastation and hopelessness in its wake. It took that women's retreat for me to finally understand how radically different God's call to exposure is. In light of the gospel, I do not have to fear exposure. Instead, God says bring all of the nooks and crannies of your sin and shame to me. Let me shine the light of the gospel into even your deepest and darkest place of fear and guilt. And when these things are exposed to the light, they first become visible. Then they become light. What radical transformation! I praise God for the humble, godly women who chose this verse for that retreat (surely with great trepidation) and then lived the beauty of this kind of exposure out before me. Instead of being devastating and degrading, we were moved by the beauty of God's power to redeem to the praise of his glorious grace.

Awake, O sleeper

The origins of the short poetic sentence in verse 14 are unknown. Stott suggests that Paul was either summarizing teaching from the Old Testament or perhaps quoting a resurrection or baptismal hymn.[56] Wherever it came from, it is a good summary of what Paul has taught in this section. Wake up! You who were dead in your trespasses and sins, arise. The same power that raised Christ from the dead is at work in you too. You who were darkness, Christ will now shine on you, exposing and redeeming that which was broken and destroyed by sin.

How do you respond to this exhortation? Do you feel threatened by this passage? Does the idea of exposing the unfruitful works of darkness make you want to hide your sin even further? The exposure of our sin is the catalyst for its transformation. Do not fear exposure, dear sister in Christ. The gospel is powerful to transform those very things you detest about yourself and your history into LIGHT. God is transforming us into his image. He does not do it by hiding our sin but exposing it and then transforming it through all he has bought for us on the cross.

---

[56] Stott, p. 201.

Reflections

Chapter 26 Ephesians 5: 15-21

15 Look carefully then how you walk, not as unwise but as wise, 16 making the best use of the time, because the days are evil. 17 Therefore do not be foolish, but understand what the will of the Lord is. 18 And do not get drunk with wine, for that is debauchery, but be filled with the Spirit, 19 addressing one another in psalms and hymns and spiritual songs, singing and making melody to the Lord with your heart, 20 giving thanks always and for everything to God the Father in the name of our Lord Jesus Christ, 21 submitting to one another out of reverence for Christ.

Look carefully how you walk

Paul has called us in the previous verses to walk as children of light. Basically, he says know who you are in Christ and then walk like it. Here, he intensifies that instruction. *Look carefully how you walk*. The Greek means to walk in a way that sees, discerns or perceives accurately, exactly, and diligently.[57] He says, furthermore, to make the most of every opportunity you have—literally to redeem or buy back the time. Strong's Concordance explains it this way.

Make wise and sacred use of every opportunity for doing good, so that zeal and well doing are as it were the purchase money by which we make the time our own.[58]

Exacting discernment and stewardship of opportunities characterizes those who are living in the light of the wisdom of God. In Colossians 4: 5, Paul says "Walk in wisdom toward outsiders, making the best use of the time." Proverbs 15 contrasts the path of those stuck in futile thought patterns with those who walk in understanding much as Paul does in Ephesians 5.

Proverbs 15:21 Folly is a joy to him who lacks sense, but a man of understanding walks straight ahead.

We defined wisdom earlier as skill in the art of gospel living. When you put it all together, instead of walking in futile thought patterns that waste instead of redeem our efforts, we are to apply ourselves at understanding God's will and his plan. We are to daily skillfully utilize the gospel in every situation we face, buying back our time by doing so.

---

[57] Strongs, s. v. "blepo akribos."
[58] Ibid, s. v. "exagorazo."

Understand what the will of the Lord is

The contrast between the foolish man who lacks sense and the man of understanding who walks in the light is stark. The foolish man represents "people who do not make a right use of their understanding, who do not see things in their true light or estimate them according to their relative importance." Paul says for us to understand God's will and walk in that way. "That is, see things as God sees them, and make his will or judgment your standard and the rule of your conduct."[59]

In Ephesians, Paul has taught us of God's plan for our salvation from before time began. We understand that we were created in the image of God and now he is conforming us back to that image, reflected perfectly in what we have seen in the life of Jesus. He has revealed to us the mystery of God's plan to reconcile both Jew and Gentile to both himself and each other. Then he showed us how this reconciliation should look in our daily lives. Through this word, we know much of the will of the Lord. God has not left us to walk aimlessly waiting for his return. He has been specific and clear with his instructions. But we are also called to pointedly engage in understanding this revelation of God. The most practical way we do this is simply through Bible study.

When I need wisdom and understanding about a particular situation, my own tendency is to go to wise Christian counselors or good Christian books first. However, this attitude works against me in the very areas I need wisdom. No Christian book can claim to be the hammer that breaks the heart of stone. No wise counselor can claim the ability to judge the unspoken attitudes of our hearts. Only God's Word has this type of power, and we must avail ourselves of his revelation to us through his written Word to understand his will. Others can speak the Word into our lives, but it is the Word itself that has the power to transform.

Be filled with the Spirit

Stott points out that "Paul has already told his readers that they have been 'sealed' with the Holy Spirit, and that they must not 'grieve' the Holy Spirit (1:13; 4:30). Now he bids them be filled with the Spirit. There is no greater secret of holiness than the infilling of him whose very nature and name are 'holy'."[60] The contrast to being drunk with wine is telling. Paul is talking about control. When someone is drunk, they have lost control to alcohol. They do things they would never do in their right mind. Paul's instructions is not just to be sober and in our right mind. He instructs us to actually be under the influence of something other than ourselves—the Holy Spirit.

Depending on your doctrinal background, you may have questions about when the Holy Spirit comes on us or wonder what the difference is between being filled and sealed with the Spirit. Remember that in Ephesians 1, Paul said that, in Christ, we are sealed with the Spirit who guarantees that God will not default on his promises to us.

---

[59] Hodge, p. 178.
[60] Stott, p. 203.

13 In him you also, when you heard the word of truth, the gospel of your salvation, and believed in him, were sealed with the promised Holy Spirit, 14 who is the guarantee of our inheritance until we acquire possession of it, to the praise of his glory.

If you are a believer, the Holy Spirit lives in you as a guarantee of your salvation. Paul teaches in Romans 8:9 that "if anyone does not have the Spirit of Christ, he does not belong to Christ." All believers have the Spirit as a seal upon their hearts. Between the time we accept Christ as our Savior and see the fulfillment of our salvation in heaven, the Spirit remains in us as God's deposit, assuring us that God *will not* default on his promises. This is a precious gift from God. He has not left us as orphans. Instead, he lives within us so that we may be confident that our relationship with him is permanent and effective.

However, while all believers are indwelt by the Holy Spirit and sealed by him, not all believers act consistently with his control. Paul exhorts believers, even though they are *sealed* with the Spirit, to also be *filled* with the Spirit. This means that we yield to him without grieving, quenching, or resisting. Remember Paul's words in Ephesians 4:29-31 on grieving the Holy Spirit?

Do not let any unwholesome talk come out of your mouths, but only what is helpful for building others up according to their needs, that it may benefit those who listen. And do not grieve the Holy Spirit of God, with whom you were sealed for the day of redemption. Get rid of all bitterness, rage and anger, brawling and slander, along with every form of malice.

We discussed this before but I will revisit it here. Paul's warning in Ephesians 4 against grieving the Spirit is given in the context of the use of angry, bitter language. Though there are many indicators of a heart that resists the Spirit versus being filled with the Spirit, the use of destructive speech in our homes, churches, marriages, and friendships is a definite red flag.

If you would like a more in depth look at the Holy Spirit, I highly recommend John Stott's short but clear book, *Baptism and Fullness of the Spirit*.

Addressing one another

Up to this point in Ephesians 5, Paul has spoken more of individual union with Christ and what it looks like to live that out practically. Now he speaks again in terms of corporate union with Christ, reminding us that we are not just members of Christ but also members of one another. We are walking this walk, not in isolation, but in worshipful union with one another. We address one another in song, corporately worshipping together, giving thanks together, and submitting to one another.

Paul speaks about this idea in Colossians 3:16 as well.

Let the word of Christ dwell in you richly, teaching and admonishing one another in all wisdom, singing psalms and hymns and spiritual songs, with thankfulness in your hearts to God.

In each case, we are addressing, teaching, and admonishing one another. I thought of this today as I participated in corporate worship during Sunday service at church. As we sang praise to God and exhortation to each other, it was encouraging to think that such mutual singing and exhortation has characterized the church since its earliest days.

Giving thanks to God and submitting to one another

This is a fitting way to end this section. The heart of this third major section of Ephesians was applying all that God has accomplished for us on the cross and walking in a way with other believers that reflects the forgiveness and reconciliation we have in him. Basically, now that you understand all that you do not deserve but have freely received in Christ, give thanks. Be humble. Submit to one another. Do not insist on your own rights. Stand down. And if you are not sure exactly how to do this in individual situations, remember that our highest standard for such humility is Jesus Christ. Study his example and learn of him.

The qualifying phrase *out of reverence for Christ* from verse 21 is important. We are not letting people walk over us out of poor self-esteem. We are not standing down because we are weary with conflict. We are not giving up because insisting on our own way seems futile. This is something altogether different. We are submitting, which Strong's defines as "a voluntary attitude of giving in, cooperating, assuming responsibility, and carrying a burden."[61] This voluntary cooperation, giving in, and carrying burdens is out of reverence for Christ. The Greek word for reverence is *phobos*, from which we get the English word phobia.[62] At the most basic level, it simply means fear. Have you gotten something about the doctrine of Christ that causes you fear, reverence, and awe? Until the truth of Paul's teaching of who Christ is and what he has accomplished for us really grips our heart at that level, we will never submit to others in the Body of Christ in the humble way God intends. We may pretend to be humble, but we will stew and become bitter. Then one day that bitterness will spew out and many will be defiled. Understand the doctrine of Ephesians 1-5, and be thankful to God in humble awe, reverence, and even fear of the one who sits in heaven with his enemies as his footstool. Praise his name corporately. Praise his name privately. Submit to one another out of reverence for him for he is worthy.

I am ending my discussion on Section 3 here. However, these are man made divisions and the ending phrase *submitting to one another out of reverence for Christ* flows directly into the new section and sets us up for Paul's final, intense stream of instructions.

Reflections

_____

_____

_____

_____

_____

_____

---

[61] Strongs, s. v. "hupotasso."
[62] Ibid, s. v. "phobos."

Section 4 Ephesians 5:22-6:24

We are now entering the final section of Ephesians, and here Paul gets more specific than ever. Paul teaches practical theology at its best, showing us exactly how all the doctrine he has taught us in Ephesians to this point makes a clear difference in the daily reality of all of our lives—husbands, wives, children, parents, workers, and bosses. This section contains the most controversial parts of the book, especially in terms of teaching to women. Before we delve into controversy, we should review the beginning of Ephesians 5 to once again make sure we have the full context of Paul's instructions.

> 1 Therefore be imitators of God, as beloved children. 2 And walk in love, as Christ loved us and gave himself up for us, a fragrant offering and sacrifice to God ... 21 submitting to one another out of reverence for Christ.

We mentioned before that Paul's "therefore" at the beginning of chapter 5 reflects immediately back on the closing words of Ephesians 4, "Be kind to one another, tenderhearted, forgiving one another, as God in Christ forgave you." Based on God's example of forgiveness to us through Christ, we are therefore to be imitators of him—walking in sacrificial love toward others just as Christ gave himself up as a sacrificial offering to God on our behalf. He is our model and the foundation of every bit of teaching that follows.

At the risk of sounding redundant, I want to reinforce verse 21, "submitting to one another out of reverence for Christ," because this is the succinct summation of all that Paul is teaching in this section. Humility and mutual submission should dominate those putting on the image of Christ. Consider once more Philippians 2: 3-8.

> 3 Do nothing from rivalry or conceit, but in humility count others more significant than yourselves. 4 Let each of you look not only to his own interests, but also to the interests of others. 5 Have this mind among yourselves, which is yours in Christ Jesus, 6 who, though he was in the form of God, did not count equality with God a thing to be grasped, 7 but made himself nothing, taking the form of a servant, being born in the likeness of men. 8 And being found in human form, he humbled himself by becoming obedient to the point of death, even death on a cross.

This is the framework on which we must hang the next controversial truths. Everything else in this section is about being imitators of God—being LIKE CHRIST—demonstrating humility and mutual submission whether you are a husband, wife, child, parent, slave, or master.

Read through Ephesians 5:21 – 6:24. Note the words or phrases that stand out to you.

Ephesians 5

[21]submitting to one another out of reverence for Christ. [22]Wives, submit to your own husbands, as to the Lord. [23]For the husband is the head of the wife even as Christ is the head of the church, his body, and is himself its Savior. [24]Now as the church submits to Christ, so also wives should submit in everything to their husbands.

[25]Husbands, love your wives, as Christ loved the church and gave himself up for her, [26]that he might sanctify her, having cleansed her by the washing of water with the word, [27]so that he might present the church to himself in splendor, without spot or wrinkle or any such thing, that she might be holy and without blemish. [28]In the same way husbands should love their wives as their own bodies. He who loves his wife loves himself. [29]For no one ever hated his own flesh, but nourishes and cherishes it, just as Christ does the church, [30]because we are members of his body. [31]"Therefore a man shall leave his father and mother and hold fast to his wife, and the two shall become one flesh." [32]This mystery is profound, and I am saying that it refers to Christ and the church. [33]However, let each one of you love his wife as himself, and let the wife see that she respects her husband.

Ephesians 6

[1]Children, obey your parents in the Lord, for this is right. [2]"Honor your father and mother" (this is the first commandment with a promise), [3]"that it may go well with you and that you may live long in the land." [4]Fathers, do not provoke your children to anger, but bring them up in the discipline and instruction of the Lord.

[5]Slaves, obey your earthly masters with fear and trembling, with a sincere heart, as you would Christ, [6]not by the way of eye-service, as people-pleasers, but as servants of Christ, doing the will of God from the heart, [7]rendering service with a good will as to the Lord and not to man, [8]knowing that whatever good anyone does, this he will receive back from the Lord, whether he is a slave or free. [9]Masters, do the same to them, and stop your threatening, knowing that he who is both their Master and yours is in heaven, and that there is no partiality with him.

[10]Finally, be strong in the Lord and in the strength of his might.

120

[11]Put on the whole armor of God, that you may be able to stand against the schemes of the devil. [12]For we do not wrestle against flesh and blood, but against the rulers, against the authorities, against the cosmic powers over this present darkness, against the spiritual forces of evil in the heavenly places. [13]Therefore take up the whole armor of God, that you may be able to withstand in the evil day, and having done all, to stand firm. [14]Stand therefore, having fastened on the belt of truth, and having put on the breastplate of righteousness, [15]and, as shoes for your feet, having put on the readiness given by the gospel of peace. [16]In all circumstances take up the shield of faith, with which you can extinguish all the flaming darts of the evil one; [17]and take the helmet of salvation, and the sword of the Spirit, which is the word of God, [18]praying at all times in the Spirit, with all prayer and supplication. To that end keep alert with all perseverance, making supplication for all the saints, [19]and also for me, that words may be given to me in opening my mouth boldly to proclaim the mystery of the gospel, [20]for which I am an ambassador in chains, that I may declare it boldly, as I ought to speak.

[21]So that you also may know how I am and what I am doing, Tychicus the beloved brother and faithful minister in the Lord will tell you everything. [22]I have sent him to you for this very purpose, that you may know how we are, and that he may encourage your hearts.

[23]Peace be to the brothers, and love with faith, from God the Father and the Lord Jesus Christ. [24]Grace be with all who love our Lord Jesus Christ with love incorruptible.

Chapter 27 Ephesians 5: 22-24

22 Wives, submit to your own husbands, as to the Lord. 23 For the husband is the head of the wife even as Christ is the head of the church, his body, and is himself its Savior. 24 Now as the church submits to Christ, so also wives should submit in everything to their husbands.

Wives, submit

Well, can it get any more controversial than that?! Is there anything other than the inerrancy of Scripture that has caused more debate and division in Christian circles in recent years? Not in my experience. Why is the idea of telling a wife she needs to submit to her husband so controversial in this day? For some of us, it is simple pride. Maybe you think your husband is unwise and will make a mess of everything if you let him. We will talk about this attitude later. But the harder truth is that there have been and still are many, many men who physically, verbally, emotionally, and/or sexually abuse women. It is clear in Scripture. It is clear in secular historical writings. It is clear in the headlines of today's newspapers. Women have rightly learned that those men cannot be trusted with authority over them.

As a disclaimer, we need to understand that this command of submission to a husband is subordinate to submission to God. This is key to distinguishing appropriate times for letting go of our rights verses times to stand against abuse. This command is not a recipe for abuse if we define abuse Biblically by God's standards of right and wrong.

We need a correct perspective on why our experience tells us it is not safe or smart for a woman to submit to her husband and why the thing to which Paul is calling us is radically different. The key is that it was the FALL OF MAN and not God's created order itself that brought about the enmity between man and woman. People who do not know Jesus can only see this issue from the perspective of depravity. They only see what is wrong with relationships between men and women, and they cling desperately to the mechanisms of self-preservation they have learned over the years. Paul calls us to look at the relationship between husband and wife as God intended it to be in perfection (he specifically refers back to creation in similar teaching in I Corinthians 11 and 1 Timothy 2). Paul has already shown us how Christ's death on the cross has purchased our redemption and begun the process of restoring us to the image of God in which we were created. Now he calls on us, male and female, to begin reflecting in our homes, not coping mechanisms for dealing with depravity, but a way of living that echoes what God intended in the perfection of his creation of man and woman.

In light of this, what does marriage that is IN CHRIST between IMITATORS OF GOD look like? Paul describes it in depth in Ephesians 5. We must include in this piece of teaching the last phrase from the previous section, which is mutual submission. Mutual, sacrificial love is the hallmark of those who are imitators of God, putting on the image of Christ through the power of our spiritual inheritance in him. At times, my husband submits his will to mine. At times, I submit my will to that of my children. And those times are not cop-outs or signs of weakness of the authority figure. Rather, it reflects the humility to which Christ has called all of us. My children want one thing. I want something else. I could insist on my own way, but as often as possible, I choose to submit my desires to theirs out of love for them that reflects the character of Christ. Sometimes, my children's desires conflict with mine in a way that I cannot compromise, and they submit to my will as their God given authority. Similarly, in those particular conflicts between a husband and a wife in which both parties hold strong differing views, God calls on the wife to submit her will.

Now back to the other argument against submission, the "my husband is unwise" argument. Maybe your husband really does have poor decision-making skills, but note that this is not about reflecting something about our husband. Verse 24 indicates this is about reflecting something about Christ and his church. There is something about submitting our will in peace and not by compulsion that reflects the cross and our spiritual inheritance. In Christ, we no longer must strive. The fate of the world or even just my little family does not depend on me either boldly taking charge or subtly manipulating. Maybe you do make better decisions than your husband, but that is irrelevant to God's purposes here. His purposes for your marriage extend WAY past the earthly cares that tend to divide us. Christ has made effective promises about what he can and will accomplish on our behalf—and when we submit our will and agenda to the imperfect authorities in our lives, we are reflecting trust not in them, but in him.

John Stott refers to I Peter 5:5 in his discussion of this section.

> Clothe yourselves, all of you, with humility toward one another, for "God opposes the proud but gives grace to the humble."

Stott then gives a beautiful, encouraging exhortation on this hard word to women.

> Should not the wife even rejoice that she has the privilege of giving a particular demonstration (of I Peter 5:5) in her attitude to her husband of the beauty of humility which is to characterize all members of God's new society? This is specially so when it is seen that her self-humbling is not coerced but free. It must have been very obvious in the ancient world. The wife had no status and few rights …. Yet the apostle addresses her as a free moral agent and calls upon her not to acquiesce in a fate she cannot escape, but to make a responsible decision before God. … Voluntary Christian self-submission is still very significant today. "Jesus Christ demonstrates rather than loses his dignity by his subordination to the Father. **When a person is voluntarily amenable to another, gives way to him, and places himself at his service, he shows greater dignity and freedom than an individual who cannot bear to be a helper and partner to anyone but himself.**"[63]

I am convicted by that last line every time I read it. I do not want to be someone who so clamors for my rights that I cannot bear to lay them down to help my husband in forbearing love like Christ.

---

[63] Stott, p. 233.

I do not want to beat a dead horse, and yet I think this passage represents such a controversial and threatening issue with women that we need to explore it deeply. I cannot get away from the universal truth governing all of us in the Body of Christ that we have already read about in I Peter 5 and Philippians 2. Loving self-sacrifice is key to being an imitator of Christ. Paul says it of himself in I Corinthians 9:19 (NAS).

For though I am free from all men, I have made myself a slave to all, so that I may win more.

As hard as it sounds, we are all called to be servants—to humbly count others more significant than ourselves; to look out not only for our own interests, but also for the interests of others. Like Christ, we are to willingly give up rights in our homes and humble ourselves in service. We are not to chafe under our God-given role, but to embrace it as the MIND OF CHRIST. Christ, GOD ALMIGHTY HIMSELF, is our example in service. Do you believe the call to be like Christ, let go of your rights, and submit yourself to another is an unfair burden for God to place on you? Or is it a blessing for you to embrace? Christ says repeatedly in the gospels that those who lose their life will find it. Those who let go of their rights and lose their vision of what the good life looks like, instead embracing God's plan for their lives, will find the overcoming abundant life to which God has called us. I have found that regular meditation on Christ's example in Philippians 2 is key to obeying God on this issue. How can I possibly submit to my husband without getting a vision for the humble, servant mind of Christ? Christ is my example.

Just in case some man is listening in on this conversation, I trust that you are not nodding your head in adamant support of these hard words toward wives. Instead, I hope you are examining yourself against Christ's example as you evaluate your own loving self-sacrifice in your home. As Jonathan Edwards put it in his *Treatise on the Religious Affections*, "False zeal is against the sin of others, while men have no zeal against their own. But he that has true zeal, exercises it chiefly against his own sins ...."[64]

In our culture, women who willingly submit their will to their husbands are assumed to be doormats. Again, Christ is our example, and even the quickest reading of the gospels shows him to be anything but a doormat. Submission does not imply that we do not have a strong, reasoned opinion. In fact, it implies the exact opposite. Consider Christ's greatest example of submission when he prays to the Father in the Garden of Gethsemane, asking to be spared the cross. He submits to the Father, saying "Not my will but yours."[65] There was a difference in desires there, and though Christ was equal with God the Father in the Trinity, his role in the Trinity was to submit to the Father.

Similarly, in our homes, there will be times where husbands and wives have strong differing opinions on a given subject. If after reasonable discussion, we cannot resolve our differing opinions, we have two options. One—we can live with the conflict, continuing to hold on to our right to our position, creating a rift in our relationship with our spouse. Or two—we can submit our will. When we have a conflict that cannot be resolved any other way, God calls Christian wives to submit to their husbands as Christ our example submitted to the Father.

---

[64] Jonathan Edwards, "Religious Affections," Christian Classics Ethereal Library, http://www.ccel.org/ccel/edwards/affections.vi.ix.html.
[65] Mark 14: 36.

As wives, we will face a lifelong battle between God's call to submit to our husbands and our inner tendency to take things into our own hands. I admit it—I am a control freak and prefer to be in charge with my agenda at the forefront. When I see that battle going on in my heart and mind, I must go back to my theology—back to what I believe about God. Manipulation, taking things into my own hands, indicates a foundation of bad theology. Perhaps I lack confidence in God's plan for my home or lack faith in God's sovereignty over my circumstances. Consider Isaiah 46.

> 9 Remember the former things, those of long ago; I am God, and there is no other; I am God, and there is none like me. 10 I make known the end from the beginning, from ancient times, what is still to come. I say: My purpose will stand, and I will do all that I please. 11 From the east I summon a bird of prey; from a far-off land, a man to fulfill my purpose. What I have said, that will I bring about; what I have planned, that will I do."

In this case, I have to ask myself, "What do I believe about God's control over situations in my home? Do I believe I can trust him without me manipulating circumstances or taking over altogether?"

The other problem I have with submission is that I often do not trust the Holy Spirit to convict my husband of sin and unwise decisions, and I think it is solely up to me to bring bad decisions on his part to his attention. Christ says of the Holy Spirit in John 16,

> 8 When he comes, he will convict the world of guilt in regard to sin and righteousness and judgment: ... 13 But when he, the Spirit of truth, comes, he will guide you into all truth. ... 14 He will bring glory to me by taking from what is mine and making it known to you.

If our husbands are in Christ, then the Holy Spirit dwells in them, and the Spirit is very good at his job of convicting man of sin and bringing to remembrance the teachings of Christ. Rather than praying to God and trusting the Spirit to convict our husbands of sin, we often become convinced that it is our responsibility to play Junior Holy Spirit, and that without our coercion, our husbands have no hope of seeing their need for change. Part of our problem here is that we tend toward a severe lack of patience. Just how long are you content to wait on the Lord to work in your spouse's life? Do you trust God with him? Do you believe God has the power to transform him? Or do you think that God cannot (or will not) do it unless you take matters into your own hands?

For a long time in my marriage, I had a profound distrust of the power of prayer and the Holy Spirit's working. As I came to know God better and understand the role of the Holy Spirit, the Lord began to transform my marriage. Instead of nagging and manipulating my husband to come around to my way of thinking, I began learning (though I still have a ways to go) to guard my tongue, pray to God, and trust the Spirit's ability to convict my husband of sin. Consistently, the Spirit has shown himself quite capable of this. Sometimes he convicts my husband. Many times he convicts me of my own wrong thinking. But opening my mouth and letting out angry, nagging, manipulative speech has never once contributed to reconciliation. In fact, as we read in Ephesians 4, that kind of angry, manipulative speech actually grieves the Spirit. Instead, I shut my mouth, pray for transformation, and rest in what I know to be true of God the Spirit.

126

Reflections

Chapter 28 Ephesians 5: 25-32

25 Husbands, love your wives, as Christ loved the church and gave himself up for her, 26 that he might sanctify her, having cleansed her by the washing of water with the word, 27 so that he might present the church to himself in splendor, without spot or wrinkle or any such thing, that she might be holy and without blemish. 28 In the same way husbands should love their wives as their own bodies. He who loves his wife loves himself. 29 For no one ever hated his own flesh, but nourishes and cherishes it, just as Christ does the church, 30 because we are members of his body. 31 "Therefore a man shall leave his father and mother and hold fast to his wife, and the two shall become one flesh." 32 This mystery is profound, and I am saying that it refers to Christ and the church.

Husbands, love

I have debated personally how much time to spend on the section of Ephesians 5 addressed specifically to husbands. My first thought was none. As I noted in the introduction to this book, I am writing this book to women. I expect some men will read it, but they are not the intended audience. I have noted in my own life that I enjoy hearing exhortations meant for my husband, but then the thoughts of what he should be doing are rolling around in my head, and I watch like an Olympic judge to see how well he is doing it. For me, this is always unhealthy and unproductive in terms of real heart change for either him or me.

However, my pastor and another godly friend (who happens to be single) both encouraged me to address this instruction. It should not take long, because the instruction is one with which we are very familiar from our study so far—love. Just as the wife is called to give a particular example of submission, the husband is called to give a particular example of love.

Love your wives. From I Corinthians 13, we know this means to be patient and kind with them, to not envy their successes or boast to them in an effort to make you look better. Do not put them down in arrogance. Do not treat them rudely or insist on your own way. Do not be irritable towards them or resentful of them. Bear their burdens and believe the best of them. Endure with them always.

Paul just said in verse 23 that the husband is the head of the wife. In Christ, the term head has a very different meaning from our culture's connotations of the word. The head of a corporation dictates terms. Employees tiptoe around them for fear of their jobs. In contrast, Jesus taught leaders to humble themselves in service. Consider Matthew 20:25-28.

25 But Jesus called them to him and said, "You know that the rulers of the Gentiles lord it over them, and their great ones exercise authority over them. 26 It shall not be so among you. But whoever would be great among you must be your servant, 27 and whoever would be first among you must be your slave, 28 even as the Son of Man came not to be served but to serve, and to give his life as a ransom for many."

Paul's instructions in Ephesians 5 reinforce this idea. The husband nourishes and cherishes his wife, sacrificing for her as Christ did.

As a single Christian woman, I longed for a husband that I thought would be a good leader, the trait I thought a godly single woman was supposed to most value. However, I was too caught up in my culture's idea of leadership to recognize the men that met God's definition. I did not recognize sacrificial servant leadership as a valuable trait. I wanted flamboyant leadership from the top. I thank God that he gave me that for which I was not looking—a husband who leads and loves through service. My husband may not fit stereotypes of the godly Christian husband, but he gets the most important thing right. He loves me as Christ loves the Church, repeatedly evident by his thoughtful acts of service to me. I am humbled tonight just meditating on acts of service he did for me in the last few hours. When married believers who are in Christ imitate God, the interplay between submission and sacrificial service is a precious treasure.

What if this kind of love is not your reality and maybe not even on your radar? My exhortation to you, single woman longing for a godly husband, is to recognize that servant leadership, love from the ground up, is the great quality for which to look in a husband. For you, married sister whose husband does not love you this way, recognize that though this may not be your reality (as it has not always been mine), it is the trajectory on which God has you. If you never on earth recognize this fully in your own life, believe that this is where we are all heading in perfection.

This mystery is profound

While we might tend to focus on instructions to husbands, the really big thing in this section is the beauty of what is revealed about the relationship Christ has with his church. Earthly husbands and wives are an imperfect picture of something deeper of eternal significance. A few weeks ago, my husband and I had a painful conversation about some hurt and concerns I had in our relationship. In that conversation, my husband was stunned that I had doubts about his love and commitment to me and told me in strong words, "You complete me!" Wow! I can say boldly that while my husband and I get many things wrong, he loves me well as Christ loves his church. I know that many beautiful godly women do not have a husband who loves them that way. I do not tell you that story to make you feel bad. Hang with me for a minute for the conclusion. After Andy told me those words, I basked in the beauty of his love for me for a while. It meant so much to me to hear him say it like that. But as I drifted off to sleep, the Spirit prompted me to think of this passage in Ephesians and it seemed he nearly audibly said to me, "Wendy, you complete me!" At first, I pushed the idea away. "No, Wendy, you do not complete Jesus!" That sounds blasphemous. That sounds like touchy, feely, emotional, Jesus-is-my-boyfriend fluff. But I kept thinking of the exact wording of this passage. Christ loved the church. He gave himself up for her. He is washing her, cleansing her, and clothing her in splendor. Christ loves the church as his own body. He nourishes and cherishes her because she is a member of his own body. The two of us, Christ and the church, have become one. I am part of this corporate thing he loves dearly and for which he gave himself completely.

The Scripture does not give me any other choice but to accept that we do indeed complete Jesus. Oh, that thought humbles me. I push it away because it conflicts with my own self-identity. I understand that Jesus is our inheritance, but understanding that we are HIS inheritance is much tougher to accept. Paul wants you and I to get this concept. You complete Jesus. He has given everything he had for you, he loves you, and he will present you spotless as part of his beautiful bride, the Church. Dear sister, whether you are loved on earth this way or not, I hope you find great peace and worth in knowing of Jesus' deep affection for and commitment to you.

Reflections

_____

_____

_____

_____

_____

_____

_____

_____

_____

_____

_____

_____

_____

_____

_____

_____

_____

_____

_____

_____

_____

Chapter 29 Ephesians 5: 33

33 However, let each one of you love his wife as himself, and let the wife see that she respects her husband.

Respect

Now back to controversial words to women. Paul has just used the same Greek word for respect, *phobeo*, in verse 21, "submitting to one another out of reverence for Christ." The Greek word means to fear, reverence, venerate, or treat with deference or reverential obedience.[66] Just in case you did not find the term *respect* itself controversial enough, consider how the Amplified Bible words this verse.

33... let the wife see that she respects and reverences her husband [that she notices him, regards him, honors him, prefers him, venerates, and esteems him; and that she defers to him, praises him, and loves and admires him exceedingly].

If you are a woman with any sense of pride, your body probably tenses with dread in the pit of your stomach as you read these words, perhaps in part because you know that *you make better decisions than your husband.*

What if you do? What if you can document that your decision-making skills are more mature and biblical than his? Does that make it unreasonable to expect you to respect your husband? Which comes first—respect or respectability? I remember an illustration given by an education professor during my undergraduate studies. He told of a junior high math teacher who, on the first day of class, mistook his students' locker numbers for their IQ's. For the entire school year, he treated the students as if they were only as smart as their locker numbers indicated. Sure enough, at the end of the year, they had consistently lived either up or down to his expectations.

This illustration reflects well on the issue at hand. If we wait until our husbands meet some subjective standard we have set for earning our respect, we will never respect them. I would be quite offended if my husband chose to not love me until I met some external criteria for being lovable. The same should be true of my respect toward him.

Surprisingly enough, I did not personally have that much of a problem with the concept of submitting to my husband. But respect was much harder. I could submit and still harbor anger and bitterness. I could still put out the vibe that says, "I am disappointed in your decision-making skills." In fact, submission without respect let me live in a delusion of self-righteousness. "I am submitting, but I do not think you know what you are doing, and I am going to continue to let you know that I do not trust you with my attitude, even though, technically, I am submitting on this

---

[66] Strongs, s. v. "phobeo."

issue." Submission does not equal respect. And submission without respect brings NO honor to God. Why would God command the combination of the two?

If you have not yet read the first three chapters of *For Women Only* by Shaunti Feldhahn, I highly recommend that you do. She has well illustrated God's wisdom in giving us the command to respect our husbands. God is the master psychologist who better understands the male/female psyche than we have any hope of comprehending, especially when it comes to the issue of respecting our husbands. The bottom line is that our husbands need our respect every bit as much as we need their love. Respect is my husband's love language. But how can we respect someone if we have deemed them unworthy of our respect? This leads back to our earlier question. Which comes first—respect or respectability? We must remember that this is God's command to wives, and God has already well earned our obedience. God has earned our respect. So we treat our husbands with deference, honoring the position in the home to which God has called them out of our respect for God. **Even if our spouse abdicates his responsibilities, when we honor him as God intended him to be, not as he is now, we are being salt and light in our homes, powerfully influencing our husbands, not by nagging and manipulating, but by humble submission to God's design.** If you want a husband you can one-day respect, I highly recommend you start treating him that way now. A godly wife's respect for her husband despite his fallen nature and tendency toward sin is a powerful tool of God to minister grace to her husband and transform him into what God intended him to be.

In summary, we are called not only to submit to our husbands but to also respond to them with respect. This is not an unfair calling. Simply put—like our husbands, we are called to be like Christ—to submit our will, humble ourselves, and take on the form of a servant in our homes. Christ is both our model and our source of strength to obey on this matter. Do you trust God's plan on this matter? Do you trust his Word? Do you trust his wisdom, sovereignty, and compassion? Are you offended that God calls you to be a servant like Christ? If you are struggling with respect and submission, start by dealing not with your views of your husband, but with your views of God himself. You can trust God with the details of your daily life. Rest in him for he is worthy.

Reflections

_____

_____

_____

_____

_____

_____

_____

_____

_____

Chapter 30 Ephesians 6: 1-4

1 Children, obey your parents in the Lord, for this is right. 2 "Honor your father and mother" (this is the first commandment with a promise), 3 "that it may go well with you and that you may live long in the land." 4 Fathers, do not provoke your children to anger, but bring them up in the discipline and instruction of the Lord.

Honor

In verse 2, Paul references Exodus 20:12, which is part of the Ten Commandments. The Greek word for honor comes from the root word *timios*, which means something that is precious and of great price, a thing that is esteemed or especially dear.[67] The Ten Commandments teach us that God values the parent/child relationship and calls us to hold it especially dear as well. The parent/child relationship is a place, much like marriage, where we believers live out much of our theology.

Exodus 20:12 is not technically the first commandment in Scripture with a promise. Rather, this is similar to the greatest commandment in Matthew 22 and Mark 12. There, a Pharisee asks Jesus what is the first commandment of all. He is not asking what was the first commandment ever written. He was asking what is the most important commandment. Similarly, "first" here in Ephesians 6:2 means of special importance. Another way to say it would be something along the lines of "a commandment with a promise of first importance." This is not the first of all commandments in importance such as the greatest command, but it is along those lines.

Obey your parents in the Lord

All of us reading this today are children. Many of us are parents. Paul brings the honoring of our parents under the umbrella of our duty to God. For many readers, this command may open more questions than answers. For several years, I worked alongside a ministry to abused women. I developed friendships with many women who were verbally, physically, or sexually abused. The majority of the time, this abuse was perpetrated by a family member, often a parent. The question arises, how do you honor a parent who betrayed a child in such a serious way? I will not attempt to tackle the complexities of a correct biblical response to familial abuse (that deserves a much more thorough treatment than I could possibly give here), but I will point out that Paul uses an important phrase here, "in the Lord". Stott says, "The latter instruction *(in the Lord)* surely modifies the former *(Children, obey your parents)*. Children are not to obey their parents in absolutely everything without exception, but in everything which is compatible with their primary loyalty,

---

[67] Strongs, s. v. "timios."

namely to their Lord Jesus Christ."[68] There are no easy answers on how exactly as adults we obey and honor our parents if they have betrayed God in sins against their children. But Paul's wording is clear that this is a command that, in Christ, is not only possible to obey, but also necessary.

Do not provoke your children

It is important to note that with each authority/submission paradigm Paul outlines (husband/wife, parent/child, master/slave), he clearly teaches mutual responsibility, reflecting back on the joint submission of chapter 5 verse 22. His instructions to parents in chapter 6 can serve as a guide to all those in authority. Paul says, "Fathers, do not provoke your children to anger." The NIV says, "Do not exasperate your children." In Colossians 3:21, Paul repeats this instruction, "Fathers, do not provoke your children, lest they become discouraged." When Paul outlines how parents should behave towards their children, note that it is "not the exercise but the RESTRAINT of their authority which he urges upon them."[69]

Paul further instructs fathers to bring up their children in the *discipline* (not punishment) and *instruction* of the Lord. Our culture has confused the terms discipline and punishment. Punishment is just retribution for sins. You get what you deserve. But what is discipline? According to *The American Heritage Dictionary* discipline is "training expected to produce a specific character or pattern of behavior, especially training that produces moral or mental improvement."[70] Punishment is reactive, while discipline is proactive. The problem is that the vast majority of us have experienced a warped form of discipline from those in authority over us and carry that baggage into our own parenting skills. It is important to understand the difference between punishment and discipline in how our Almighty Father treats his children. From there, we can get a right view of how we are to treat our own.

According to Romans 8:1, Christ bore the full weight of our punishment for sin on the cross, and we are no longer condemned for our sin. This is the very good news of the gospel! Then in Romans 8:29, we learn that God's plan from before time began was to transform us into the likeness of his Son. This is why we need discipline (i.e. training in righteousness).

> 1 Therefore, there is now no condemnation for those who are in Christ Jesus, 2 because through Christ Jesus the law of the Spirit of life set me free from the law of sin and death….29 For those God foreknew he also predestined to be conformed to the likeness of his Son….

Instead of punishing us for our sins, God the Father poured out his full wrath for our sins on Jesus at the cross. Now, God disciplines us to mold us into the image of his Son. Grace and mercy dominate his plan for training us in righteousness, and his methods should dominate ours as we train our own children. I love how the King James Version translates verse 4—bring up your children "in the nurture and admonition of the Lord." I do not automatically associate the term *discipline* with *nurture*—but the Bible does. I need to understand God's view of discipline and

---

[68] Stott, p. 242.
[69] Ibid, p. 245.
[70] *The American Heritage Dictionary of the English Language*, 4th ed., s. v. "discipline."

nurture. His instructions to discipline/nurture our children reflect directly back on the methods Christ uses with us, his Body, which we just studied in Ephesians 5.

Ephesians 5:29 For no one ever hated his own flesh, but nourishes and cherishes it, just as Christ does the church,

My boys are fairly young as I write this book. I am a novice parent only just beginning to ponder what gospel-centered parenting looks like in our home. I struggle daily with the desire to control my children's actions at the expense of their heart. The patience, grace, and kindness of God toward his children constantly amaze me as I ponder my own impatience with my mere two children. It convicts and inspires me as well. Meditating on his example to me is my primary hope for nurturing and instructing my own children well. I must parent my children the way God parents his.

Reflections

_____

_____

_____

_____

_____

_____

_____

_____

_____

_____

_____

_____

_____

_____

_____

_____

_____

_____

_____

Chapter 31 Ephesians 6: 5-9

5 Slaves, obey your earthly masters with fear and trembling, with a sincere heart, as you would Christ, 6 not by the way of eye-service, as people-pleasers, but as servants of Christ, doing the will of God from the heart, 7 rendering service with a good will as to the Lord and not to man, 8 knowing that whatever good anyone does, this he will receive back from the Lord, whether he is a slave or free.

9 Masters, do the same to them, and stop your threatening, knowing that he who is both their Master and yours is in heaven, and that there is no partiality with him.

Rendering service as to the Lord

Here is another potentially controversial section of Paul's teaching in Ephesians. I trust that all those reading this book believe that slavery is an unjust system inconsistent with Christian beliefs. Slavery in the Bible was very different than our concept of modern slavery as practiced in the United States. In Scripture, it was more like indentured servitude. Regardless, does the fact that we believe slavery to be unjust mean that this teaching is irrelevant? Certainly not, for there remains a multitude of oppressive, unjust circumstances affecting Christians around the world. Often, disagreeing with the system and protesting its unrighteousness makes little impact on the day-to-day situation in which those who are oppressed find themselves. Paul teaches here that the gospel of Jesus, our spiritual inheritance, and all the ramifications of it **equip us to live righteously in unrighteous situations.** In Christ, you can be both oppressed and blessed! Obedience is not contingent upon two parties both handling their responsibilities righteously. We can be obedient to God even when others treat us in unrighteous ways. This is part of the hope of our inheritance in Christ. I am not dependent on my fellow man's obedience for me to live righteously.

Furthermore, I must guard myself against focusing primarily on the requirements of the other party in my conflict. The unrighteous tend to focus on the Biblical obligations of others. Masters like instructions to slaves. Slaves focus on instructions to masters. Husbands like instructions to wives, and wives like those to husbands. But Paul calls ALL of us to accountability for ourselves. Everyone is called to be imitators of Christ—wives reflecting the submission and humility of Christ; husbands reflecting Christ's self-sacrificing love for his church; slaves serving as Christ did, washing the feet of his disciples; masters called to reflect the same thing back to their slaves.

These particular instructions to slaves are inspiring and hopeful. Paul says to obey sincerely as to the Lord and not to men. We are called to serve with pure motives, once again letting go of our rights and allowing our view of God's kingdom purposes to give perspective to oppressive circumstances. When God's eternal plan is the filter through which we view our circumstances, then and only then can we *render service with a good will*, believing that *whatever good anyone does, this he will receive back from the Lord.*

Masters, do the same

Once again, Paul's instructions to authorities are counter to our (and his) culture's view of authority. Paul says for masters to do the same as he just instructed to slaves—to serve sincerely as you would the Lord Himself, with good will, believing that you will receive back from the Lord a blessing for this sacrificial service. As Stott noted with parents and we saw also with husbands, Paul repeatedly emphasizes the restraint of authority. The authority figure becomes the servant if he wants to lead like Christ.

Reflections

_____
_____
_____
_____
_____
_____
_____
_____
_____
_____
_____
_____
_____
_____
_____
_____
_____
_____
_____
_____
_____

Chapter 32 Ephesians 6: 10-20

We are ready to tackle the concluding group of teaching from Ephesians. This is the grand finale to all we have discussed from the beginning of chapter 1 to this point. We were created as image bearers of God. At the fall of man, sin and depravity corrupted God's creation. It affected every aspect of our lives—family, church, culture, politics. Every piece of our lives is warped far away from the image of God through the fall of man. But in Ephesians 1 and 2, we start to see the beauty of God's plan to get it back. He is calling us back to what he created us to be, and he has accomplished something on the cross deep and transforming that equips us to do so. Then in Ephesians 3 through 5, we see that we are equipped to live not in the inheritance of the fall of man but in light of our creation as imitators of God. Now through our inheritance in Christ, we start to reclaim the image of God in our homes, our churches, and our culture.

This all leads to Paul's final exhortation—a strongly worded admonition to go and live this out in the midst of the battles of life.

10 Finally, be strong in the Lord and in the strength of his might. 11 Put on the whole armor of God, that you may be able to stand against the schemes of the devil. 12 For we do not wrestle against flesh and blood, but against the rulers, against the authorities, against the cosmic powers over this present darkness, against the spiritual forces of evil in the heavenly places. 13 Therefore take up the whole armor of God, that you may be able to withstand in the evil day, and having done all, to stand firm. 14 Stand therefore, having fastened on the belt of truth, and having put on the breastplate of righteousness, 15 and, as shoes for your feet, having put on the readiness given by the gospel of peace. 16 In all circumstances take up the shield of faith, with which you can extinguish all the flaming darts of the evil one; 17 and take the helmet of salvation, and the sword of the Spirit, which is the word of God, 18 praying at all times in the Spirit, with all prayer and supplication. To that end keep alert with all perseverance, making supplication for all the saints, 19 and also for me, that words may be given to me in opening my mouth boldly to proclaim the mystery of the gospel, 20 for which I am an ambassador in chains, that I may declare it boldly, as I ought to speak.

Finally

This is Paul's final exhortation—to go out in awareness and apply all he has taught us up to this point. Satan is scheming. Paul refers to it as the *schemes of the devil* and the *fiery darts of the evil one*. Satan is not merely powerful and wicked, but he is also crafty and deceptive with plans to undermine and destroy what God is doing in our lives. If we were not in Christ, there would be nothing to do but be terrified.

Even now there is probably an email waiting in your inbox or a voicemail on your phone that represents the schemes of Satan to snatch any seeds sown through this study. I have led a number of women's retreats, always finding the time away with other women in Christ a wonderful blessing. But inevitably, Satan executes on his schemes to snatch my joy the moment the retreat is over. One year in particular, on the way home from an especially spiritually encouraging time, the first voicemail on my cell phone was my neighbor asking me why there was an ambulance in my yard. After finally getting my husband on the phone, I found out that he was okay, but that we needed to take him to the emergency room as soon as I got home due to some heart issues he was experiencing. It ended up being relatively minor, but we spent the night in the hospital before we figured it all out. I recounted this to an elder at church afterwards, and he shared with me a long list of experiences he had as a youth pastor after returning from spiritually refreshing times away. His wife called it "re-entry." They grew to expect joy robbers, those land mines placed by the enemy to blow up all the good that had been sown. Flat tires, children who had to go to the ER after swallowing chicken bones, students whose parents split up during the weekend they were away—these were some of their personal experiences returning from times away of spiritual refreshment. Satan is very resourceful, and he often plans his most strategic attacks when we are coming down from periods of great blessing and growth.

Paul was aware of Satan's schemes. He had lived under Satan's fiery darts for many years and wanted the Ephesians to be equipped for battle. For us today, the moments away at a retreat or in fruitful personal study of Scripture are not the crucial moments of battle with Satan. The battle comes when you put the book down, walk out the church doors, or return from the retreat and reengage with life. If this particular study has been meaningful to you, I guarantee that Satan will quickly send his best schemes to snatch the seeds sown through it.

Stand firm

Paul wants you and I well equipped and confident to face such attacks. He says to be strong and to stand firm. This is war, and the most important thing in war is to stand in place and not give ground. He is summoning us to the fight of our life until Jesus returns. Why are we in this war if Christ has already defeated principalities and put all things under his feet as Paul described in Ephesians 1? Paul has consistently presented throughout Ephesians the tension between our eternal spiritual reality and our temporary earthly reality. God allows us, even calls us, to participate in the things he does on our behalf, and spiritual warfare is the culmination of that participation. **The present conflict is real though the final result is certain.** We know what God has eternally secured for us in heaven, and yet he still does not allow us to remain passive observers on the sideline.

We do not wrestle against flesh and blood

Before we delve further into the war analogy, I want to make sure we are talking about it with the right foundation. I have heard much talk of war in the Christian church over the years. Many times that rhetoric is testosterone driven nonsense used to wage war against specific people. The first thing that Paul does here is to clearly identify our enemy. You need to understand against whom you are to stand firm. This is foundational to every thing else that he instructs. Verse 12 specifically defines our adversary.

142

12 For we do not wrestle against flesh and blood, but against the rulers, against the authorities, against the cosmic powers over this present darkness, against the spiritual forces of evil in the heavenly places.

I cannot over emphasize how important it is that we understand and appropriate this truth. We are not wrestling with people. We are wrestling with spiritual forces in the heavenly places. **When Satan gets us to take our war against each other, he has won exactly the ground he wanted.** Consider Paul's instructions in 2 Timothy 2:24-26.

24 And the Lord's servant must not be quarrelsome but kind to everyone, able to teach, patiently enduring evil, 25 correcting his opponents with gentleness. God may perhaps grant them repentance leading to a knowledge of the truth, 26 and they may come to their senses and escape from the snare of the devil, after being captured by him to do his will.

Paul says that when you are in a conflict with a person do not attack the person. Even if you believe they are Satan's emissaries, you respond to them with kindness, patience, and gentle correction because they are ensnared by Satan. Our desire should be to minister gospel grace to them that they may escape him. This person is not your enemy. They are a prisoner of your enemy. We must keep that straight. It is ridiculous to think we can win a battle with an enemy by attacking his prisoners, but we do it all the time in the church.

Whole Armor of God

Once we understand the enemy, how do we do effective battle with Satan? Paul is giving more than a pep talk to boost morale. He is giving us concrete tools in our battle with Satan, what he calls the whole armor of God. Depending on your history in the church, you may or may not be familiar with this concept. Having been raised in the church, I have heard about the whole armor of God in various settings over the years. The problem was I only heard it quoted in context of this one little piece of Ephesians 6. However, I have come to understand this armor in a radically different way now that I have studied it in context of Ephesians 1 through 5. When Paul talks about putting on the whole armor of God, he is talking about it in context of everything he has already taught us in earlier chapters—our adoption into God's family and spiritual inheritance in Christ; our reconciliation with both God and his people through Christ; the unity and diversity we have in Christ's body; and the hope we have in our homes, churches, and even oppressive workplaces when we become imitators of God.

Note that this is the armor of God. He is the original wearer of this armor, as seen in prophecies of Jesus in Isaiah.

Isaiah 11:5 Righteousness shall be the belt of his waist, and faithfulness the belt of his loins.

Isaiah 59:17 He put on righteousness as a breastplate, and a helmet of salvation on his head; he put on garments of vengeance for clothing, and wrapped himself in zeal as a cloak.

It is interesting that on this side of the cross, instead of garments of vengeance, we now wear the gospel of peace. We will talk more about that in a moment. Right now, I want to focus on the fact that Jesus is the first wearer of this armor and now we are instructed, once more, to be like him. This reminds me once again of our union with Christ. We are IN HIM. Whatever is true of Christ is connected to his people as well. As we walk through the individual pieces of the armor of God, they directly parallel Jesus' own example to us. Once again, it is enough that we be like him.

Belt of truth

The first piece of armor Paul mentions is the "belt of truth". The use of the term *belt* speaks to readiness and preparedness. Consider Exodus 12:11

> In this manner you shall eat it: with your belt fastened, your sandals on your feet, and your staff in your hand. And you shall eat it in haste. It is the LORD's Passover.

They were to be ready to go—with their belt fastened to hold up their tunic, shoes on their feet, and their staff in hand. In our case, the belt that readies us is the belt of truth. Truth prepares us for the entire Christian life. We must know the truth in order to accurately serve and care for others. There should be no dichotomy in the church—some pursuing truth while others do service. The truth of Scripture is the thing that equips the man or woman of God to competently navigate every good work to which God has called them (2 Timothy 3:16-17). Satan is known throughout Scripture as a liar. Implicit in the idea of the belt of truth is that you know the truth from Scripture that can cut through Satan's lies. I have only touched briefly on this concept here. The issue of spiritual truth is closely tied to the sword of the Spirit, and we will look at this idea in more depth there.

Breastplate of righteousness

Righteousness. Holiness. Obedience. These are words that are not naturally well received by any human. They actually can be quite threatening. Talk to me about grace or love, but do not talk to me about righteousness. However, Paul has set us up well through the first five chapters of Ephesians to hear this message now the way God intended it. God does not save us BY our obedience, but he does save us FOR our obedience. Though the concepts of righteousness, obedience, and holiness have been well abused by religious legalists of every persuasion, we cannot give these words over to them and lose their true meaning and God's good plan for the righteousness of his children.

In God's design, righteousness and holiness mean at the most basic level simply following God and being like him. He is both the definition of what it means to be righteous and the channel by which we obey him. He is the means and the end. His yoke is easy, and his burden is light (Matthew 11:30). If you are weighed down by the idea of righteousness, you have let the wrong people define the term for you.

In Zechariah 3, we get a vision of the battle with Satan as he accuses Joshua.

144

1 Then he showed me Joshua the high priest standing before the angel of the LORD, and Satan standing at his right hand to accuse him. 2 And the LORD said to Satan, "The LORD rebuke you, O Satan! The LORD who has chosen Jerusalem rebuke you! Is not this a brand plucked from the fire?" 3 Now Joshua was standing before the angel, clothed with filthy garments. 4 And the angel said to those who were standing before him, "Remove the filthy garments from him." And to him he said, "Behold, I have taken your iniquity away from you, and I will clothe you with pure vestments." 5 And I said, "Let them put a clean turban on his head." So they put a clean turban on his head and clothed him with garments. And the angel of the LORD was standing by.

Satan's primary accusation against Joshua is refuted by God clothing him in his own pure clothing. Consider also Isaiah 61:10.

> I will greatly rejoice in the LORD;
>   my soul shall exult in my God,
>   for he has clothed me with the garments of salvation;
>   he has covered me with the robe of righteousness,
> as a bridegroom decks himself like a priest with a beautiful headdress,
>   and as a bride adorns herself with her jewels.

We have these garments because God has purchased them for us, and we need to put them on in the face of Satan's ever present schemes and accusations against us. This means remembering the gospel, or wearing the gospel if you will. You are now clothed in Christ's righteousness in place of your own filthy rags, and no one can rip them off. This breastplate of righteousness will defend you from much of Satan's deceptive attempts to undermine your growth in Christ and effectiveness in his Body.

Gospel of peace

Paul words his next exhortation in an interesting way, "as shoes for your feet, having put on the readiness given by the gospel of peace." John Stott calls this our "gospel boots", referring to the sturdy, open toed half boots worn by Roman soldiers.[71] I am intrigued by several parts of how Paul words this. First, there is a readiness given to us by the gospel of *peace*. The term peace sticks out to me like a sore thumb in this warfare scenario. So far, Paul has used a hard-core, defensive weapon analogy to get his point across about the seriousness of this war. But now he says peace— which we defined in section 1 as the absence of the rage and havoc of war.

Put together the idea of peace with the picture of shoes. There are two ways of viewing the use of the term shoes. First, there are several places in Scripture where shoes or feet refer to the proclaiming of the good news of the gospel. Paul quotes Nahum 1:15 and Isaiah 52:7 in Romans 10:15 when he says

> And how are they to preach unless they are sent? As it is written, "How beautiful are the feet of those who preach the good news!"

---

[71] Stott, p. 279.

This proclamation of the good news of peace really sticks out in the context of war. Paul says stand firm. Do not give ground. Because you have a message of peace and reconciliation! We are preaching the end of the very conflict we are fighting. We are preaching the end of this war!

I believe there is a second figurative value of associating the gospel of peace with shoes for my feet. Not just are we proclaiming the gospel of peace to our enemies, we proclaim it also to ourselves. There is something about this gospel of peace that makes us ready or prepared for Satan's plots against us.[72]

As I preach the gospel of peace to myself, the modern phrase "getting my toes stepped on" comes to mind. My feet are sensitive, and I have a long-standing, somewhat neurotic fear of someone running over my feet from behind with a grocery cart. Figuratively, I often get my toes stepped on. By this I mean that I am sensitive and get my feelings hurt easily. This is a place that Satan often attacks me. I am sure you too know people whose feelings are so easily hurt that you cannot tell them anything, and yet can you admit to yourself that many times that person is you?

Personally, I truly do want to know the hard truths about myself. If I have a sinful habit that wounds others, I want to know about it and change. Yet I am so sensitive that I get my feelings hurt way before I can hear the truth. To quote Jack Nicholson in *A Few Good Men*, "You can't handle the truth." I have found it a terrible hindrance to growth in Christ to be unable to bear confrontation from another who can clearly see my sin. I have told my husband that I want his honest feedback, but his reply is that I am often so sensitive he cannot tell me anything. The gospel of peace has something for me in that moment. When I receive either helpful or hurtful criticism, there is something about the gospel of peace that readies me when I apply it in that moment. It protects me from Satan's attempts to undermine my growth. How?

I tend to attach my identity to whatever positive affirmation I get from someone, either my husband at home or others in ministry. I have been convicted that Jesus' affirmation, "Well done thou good and faithful servant," is often not good enough for me. That happens when my spiritual reality, those things secured for me eternally in the heavenly places, is not real to me. I have had to learn to meditate on Jesus' "Well done" as the affirmation that seals my identity. I should not need constant affirmation from other people in order for me to walk forward. When I am dependent on earthly affirmation, I either walk forward proudly expecting compliments, or I become paralyzed and do not walk at all because I fear condemnation.

The gospel of peace equips me to find my security and identity in what Christ has accomplished for me on the cross. He is the vine, I am the branch, and apart from him I can do nothing. At the same time, anything good that I do, he gets the glory. If that is my mentality, then feedback, even negative feedback meant in hurtful ways, does not have to shake my confidence in my identity in Christ.

I have given a particular personal application of the protection afforded by these gospel boots. The way the gospel of peace prepares us for spiritual combat and protects us in the battle is worthy of long meditation. It speaks to the core of who we are and how we see ourselves in relation to God and others.

---

[72] Strongs, s. v. "hetoimasia."

Reflections

Chapter 33 Ephesians 6: 10-20 continued

Shield of Faith

Next, Paul exhorts us to take up the shield of faith in all circumstances. With this shield of faith, we can extinguish all the flaming darts of the wicked one. The picture is of the Roman soldiers dipping their shields in water, which would then extinguish flaming arrows shot at them by the enemy. This phrase raises the question, "What exactly is faith?" Thankfully, Scripture clearly defines faith for us in Hebrews 11:1-6.

1 Now faith is the assurance of things hoped for, the conviction of things not seen. 2 For by it the people of old received their commendation. 3 By faith we understand that the universe was created by the word of God, so that what is seen was not made out of things that are visible.

4 By faith Abel offered to God a more acceptable sacrifice than Cain, through which he was commended as righteous, God commending him by accepting his gifts. And through his faith, though he died, he still speaks. 5 By faith Enoch was taken up so that he should not see death, and he was not found, because God had taken him. Now before he was taken he was commended as having pleased God. 6 And without faith it is impossible to please him, for whoever would draw near to God must believe that he exists and that he rewards those who seek him.

The first part of faith found in Hebrews 11: 1 is that it is **not sight**. It is hope for and conviction of things that are not seen. If you can see it, it is not faith. The whole point of faith is that you believe something that your external reality is not reinforcing for you at that moment. There are fiery darts, evil schemes, and chaos surrounding you. The shield of faith is that I believe in a heavenly reality in which things are going on that I cannot see that dictate how I view my personal chaos. My spiritual reality in heaven changes how I interpret my circumstances even though I cannot physically see these truths right now.

According to Hebrews 11:6, there are two particular aspects of this faith. We must first believe that God exists. I do not see God physically in this location right now, but I believe that God is real, that he exists. Second, I must believe that he rewards those who diligently seek him. He is good to his children. This is my shield of faith. No matter what my chaos, I know my eternal reality, and I am determined in Christ to translate the chaos in my life in terms of what I know to be true about God. Nothing protects you from Satan's fiery arrows like knowing what you believe and interpreting your circumstances in light of that eternal truth.

The helmet of salvation

The helmet covers the head. Paul instructs us to "put on" this helmet, which indicates once again that there is something we need to appropriate here. Paul gives similar instructions in I Thessalonians 5:8.

> But since we belong to the day, let us be sober, having put on the breastplate of faith and love, and for a helmet the hope of salvation.

Here, he speaks of the hope of salvation since we belong to the day (of Christ). This hope is our earnest expectation of and confidence in our destiny in Christ. In 2 Corinthians 4, Paul speaks of how our outer man is decaying but our inner man is being renewed day by day.

> 7 But we have this treasure (the glory of God through the face of Jesus) in jars of clay, to show that the surpassing power belongs to God and not to us. 8 We are afflicted in every way, but not crushed; perplexed, but not driven to despair; 9 persecuted, but not forsaken; struck down, but not destroyed....

> 16 So we do not lose heart. Though our outer self is wasting away, our inner self is being renewed day by day. 17 For this light momentary affliction is preparing for us an eternal weight of glory beyond all comparison, 18 as we look not to the things that are seen but to the things that are unseen. For the things that are seen are transient, but the things that are unseen are eternal.

There is undeniably a great contrast between what God has promised is going on inside of us and in heaven for us with what we often experience in our earthly reality. The helmet of salvation represents our hope. We must filter all of our current realities through that hope or confident expectation of rescue and reconciliation for eternity. This helmet protects our most vulnerable places.

The sword of the Spirit

The Word of God is the sword of the Spirit, and it is the only offensive weapon in this whole section. What does this phrase mean? It is not just a cheap phrase to throw around to sound spiritual, though that often happens in Christian circles. Instead, this phrase reflects the truth of God's work for our benefit through his written word. Elsewhere, Scripture calls the Word of God a double-edged sword.

> Hebrews 4:12 For the word of God is living and active, sharper than any two-edged sword, piercing to the division of soul and of spirit, of joints and of marrow, and discerning the thoughts and intentions of the heart.

The written Word is the sword of the Spirit that pierces our hearts and judges the motives and thoughts in the core of our being, well hidden from others but not from God. And the Word of God is LIVING. That is why words written thousands of years ago can meet you personally today in a way that is real and relevant to your needs. We are not talking about quoting a Shakespearean sonnet that gives you minimal comfort. We are not reading a book in which we can generally identify with the protagonist. Instead, when we read the Bible, we are reading something written by an eternal sovereign God who has a supernatural ability to manipulate it and apply it in a way like he wrote it directly to you for the circumstances you find yourself in on this particular day. The Word of God is his sword through which he cuts us open, reveals our hearts, and shows us himself.

As I mentioned earlier, this armor is God's, and he wore it first. Jesus is our example on how to use the double-edged sword of the Word against our enemy Satan. Consider Jesus' temptation in Matthew 4. Three times Satan tempts Jesus, and each time Jesus responds, "It is written …" In every accusation and temptation, Jesus responds with specific Scripture, and it works! Satan is refuted and gives up his efforts in that setting.

Allow me to apply this particular spiritual weapon to the specific sin issue we talked about from Ephesians 5, sexual sin and addiction. Walking forward in forgiveness of such sin is a daily battle. We *are* forgiven. Jesus' punishment upon the cross bought us peace, and by his wounds, we are HEALED. Yet, Satan is the accuser, and he lives to remind us of the shame and guilt of our sin. Satan whispers, "Yeah, Christ died for you, but that is not enough to really heal you." Satan's life goal is for us to believe this lie because it makes the cross look ineffective.

How do we battle Satan the Accuser? We must use our spiritual sword against his schemes. Combine that with 2 Corinthians 10:5 in which Paul exhorts us to recognize deceptive thought patterns, take them captive, and make them submit to what we know to be true about God. When Satan accuses you, tempting you to fall back into old mental patterns, Scripture is the one weapon that has always defeated him.

"You are worthless." NO! I have been adopted into God's family and given the amazing title of co-heir with Jesus Christ (Romans 8:17).

"You are doomed to repeat your past behavior." NO! God has not only begun a good work in me, but he promises to continue transforming me until the day I am presented as the spotless Bride of Christ in heaven (Philippians 1:6).

"You will always be a sexual addict even if you don't act on it." NO! By His wounds I am HEALED (Isaiah 53:5).

Reflections

_____

_____

_____

_____

_____

_____

Chapter 34 Ephesians 6: 18-20

18 praying at all times in the Spirit, with all prayer and supplication. To that end keep alert with all perseverance, making supplication for all the saints, 19 and also for me, that words may be given to me in opening my mouth boldly to proclaim the mystery of the gospel, 20 for which I am an ambassador in chains, that I may declare it boldly, as I ought to speak.

<u>*Praying*</u>

Though I am starting a new chapter on this section of Ephesians 6, it is important to note that this is simply Paul's conclusion to his teaching on the armor of God. He is not starting a new thought or new instruction. He has not even begun a new sentence. He is simply finishing his last point. These three verses are the grand finale to his instructions on spiritual warfare. Prayer is crucial to standing firm in the war with Satan. Pray at all times, for all the saints, with all prayer and supplication. Prayer is THAT necessary to the battle.

You might be concerned with Paul's instruction to pray at all times. That bothered me for many years because it seemed something totally unattainable to me. Surely Paul does not literally mean at all times, does he?! Consider also I Thessalonians 5.

16 Be joyful always; 17 pray continually; 18 give thanks in all circumstances, for this is God's will for you in Christ Jesus.

Does that sound like a heavy burden? Does God really expect me to talk with him all day? I have groceries to buy, kids to feed, tests for which to study, and bosses to please. I do not have time to pray all day long. If you think that way, remember what we learned about our union with Christ in earlier chapters. You and I are *in* Christ and commanded to *abide* with Christ. Christ is the Head and we are his Body. When we are at the grocery store, school, home, or work, we are supernaturally connected with Christ all day, every day. We have God Almighty living in us as the Spirit, and we are called to reflect this reality and take advantage of it in the form of prayer. Sometimes it will be a gushing river of conversation with God flowing through the forefront of our minds. Sometimes it will be a quiet stream of meditation and rest in the background of our minds. Regardless, we should always walk mindful of God's presence. We all know what it is like to have something continually on our mind all day. Well, God is to be continually on our mind. We are called to continually acknowledge and take advantage of the supernatural union we have with God Almighty.

The issue is not that we bring God our laundry list lest he be unaware of our needs. No, God allows us to bring him our requests more for our peace of mind. Philippians 4:6-7 says

Do not be anxious about anything, but in everything, by prayer and petition, with thanksgiving, present your requests to God. And the peace of God, which transcends all understanding, will guard your hearts and your minds in Christ Jesus.

God invites us to bring our requests to him because time spent in his presence in prayer is a means of experiencing his grace. God promises supernatural peace to stabilize our hearts and minds when we bring our needs to him. We do not bring our needs to him for his benefit but for ours.

The final phrase in Christ's instructive prayer in Matthew 6:13 is "lead us not into temptation, but deliver us from evil." We often make the mistake of thinking that while Christ was fully responsible for our rescue from sin at our salvation, it is now up to us to figure out how to battle temptation the rest of our lives. Paul has taught us throughout Ephesians something entirely different. We are utterly dependent on God in our battle to put to death our sinful desires and grow more and more like Christ. Paul encourages the Corinthians with this truth:

I Corinthians 10:13 No temptation has overtaken you but such as is common to man; and God is faithful, who will not allow you to be tempted beyond what you are able, but with the temptation will provide the way of escape also, so that you will be able to endure it.

Our battle with temptation by Satan is a joint venture with God. 2 Peter 2:9 teaches that "the Lord knows how to rescue the godly from temptation…." After salvation, you and I are no longer slaves to sin. God promises that when we are presented with a temptation to sin, he will provide a way of escape that we may bear it. He makes the way of escape, and we are obligated to walk closely with him that we might both recognize and take advantage of the escape he provides for us. We are dependent upon God in prayer for this. We cannot overcome sin in the Christian life apart from continually seeking out God's presence in prayer.

When we are overcome with fear and worry, how often do we seek out friends, family, or church leaders to unburden ourselves? We feel this overwhelming need to pour out our hearts to someone, but we so often ignore the *One* to whom we should be pouring out our hearts. Pouring out your requests before God is the number one way to deal with vexing issues. It is the most effective way to mentally deal with your burdens. You cannot do spiritual battle with Satan without it.

As we conclude this section on spiritual warfare, I hope we will take seriously these weapons God has given us—the belt of truth, shield of faith, breastplate of righteousness, gospel of peace, sword of the Spirit, and prayer. How does this look for you? As I walk forward through each stressful daily circumstance, I am learning to stop in that moment to ask myself, "How does the gospel of peace equip me to deal with this conflict? What has God purchased on the cross that enables me to be at peace with him and others in circumstances that are driving me crazy? What does the sword of the Spirit tell me is the truth? How does my view of my circumstances change when I view it through the lens of faith in God?" The good news of the gospel and the spiritual benefits that are available to us through it are real and tangible. God reminds me as I look to him, "I raised Christ from the dead and THAT power is at work on your behalf. Avail yourself of it. I

am the vine you are the branches. I am the Head and you are the Body. Walk forward in peace."
And he transforms how I respond to my stressful circumstances. Most of the time, the situation does not go away, but my stressful reaction to it is transformed as I refocus on my heavenly reality and interpret my earthly circumstances through that lens.

Sometimes our circumstances are intense. Other times they are relatively mild. But our spiritual inheritance in Christ is equally relevant to both types of struggles. When we are well armored through our knowledge of all we have in Christ, it protects our head, breast, and feet from Satan's fiery darts. He is ineffective at getting us to disbelieve that God is good to his children, that he has stored up for us supernatural blessings, and that we have the power of the resurrection at work in us as we face it all.

This is what equips us to go forward, be strong, and stand firm.

Reflections

Chapter 35 Ephesians 6: 21-24

21 So that you also may know how I am and what I am doing, Tychicus the beloved brother and faithful minister in the Lord will tell you everything. 22 I have sent him to you for this very purpose, that you may know how we are, and that he may encourage your hearts. 23 Peace be to the brothers, and love with faith, from God the Father and the Lord Jesus Christ. 24 Grace be with all who love our Lord Jesus Christ with love incorruptible.

Paul has written a great symphony on the gospel. The last section was the climax and now the music calms in closing. With his salutations of peace, love, faith, and grace, Paul's final words bring us full circle to the beginning of this letter. In the first section of this book, I told you that John Stott believed that much of the message of Ephesians was summed up in the phrase, *peace through grace.* I believe Paul's use of these terms again in the closing notes of this grand epistle is reason for us to consider them one final time.

Grace

The common theme of all the varied definitions that I have read of grace is that grace is not about giving what is due. *Charis*, the Greek word translated grace in Ephesians, is also used in Luke 6 when Jesus teaches a pivotal piece of the good news of the gospel.[73]

32 If you love those who love you, what *benefit* is that to you? For even sinners love those who love them. 33 And if you do good to those who do good to you, what *benefit* is that to you? For even sinners do the same. 34 And if you lend to those from whom you expect to receive, what *credit* is that to you? Even sinners lend to sinners, to get back the same amount. 35 But love your enemies, and do good, and lend, expecting nothing in return, and your reward will be great, and you will be sons of the Most High, for he is kind to the ungrateful and the evil. 36 Be merciful, even as your Father is merciful.

As I said in the opening chapter of this study, Jesus points out that when you give back what is earned or deserved, it is not *charis*—it is not grace. It is not favor or benefit, and it is not credited to you as anything other than exactly what you are expected to do. Instead, grace does what is unexpected and undeserved. It is an unreasonably good response. When we give grace, this undeserved favor that does good to enemies and lends expecting nothing in return, then we give evidence to our relationship with our Father in heaven, because THIS is his calling card. He is kind to the ungrateful and evil. He is full of grace.

---

[73] Strongs, s. v. "charis."

In Luke 6, Jesus says the evidence of our understanding of God's grace toward us is OUR GRACE TOWARD OTHERS. Paul has taught us throughout Ephesians the exact same thing. First you get the gospel, God's grace to you to the praise of his glory, and then you go live it out in relationship with others. Grace and humility are intertwined theological concepts. When we get grace, the only choice is humility. In Christian circles, we sometimes mistake other virtues for grace and humility. We admire Christians who are diplomatic, generally friendly, or polite. But those traits, while pleasant at times, are not the same as grace and the humility that follows it. Grace is an unreasonably lavish response to those undeserving of it, and it is based on our own understanding of God's great, undeserved favor toward us. **If grace does not dominate your understanding of your relationship to God and your obligations to others, your religion will suck the life out of you and others around you.**

Peace

I said it in the first section, and I will repeat it again here. I painfully long for peace—peace from war, peace in my racially diverse community, peace in my family, and peace between Christian brothers and sisters who bite and devour each other when they should be each other's best advocates. Paul has given us the key for unlocking the gift of peace for my family, my church, and my community. It is grace, and he has spent many words in Ephesians to make sure I understand the connection between grace, peace, and God's good plan for reconciling us to himself and each other.

Sister in Christ, I can come up with no better summary than Stott for all Paul has taught us through Ephesians. *Peace through grace.* Do you want that? Does that phrase evoke hope in you for the future? Do you feel equipped now to walk forward in these things to which God has called us? Remember, both Paul's and Jesus' examples teach us this is not peace FROM trials, but peace THROUGH trials. I hope you, like me, have been challenged by the Word to pursue gospel reconciliation in your relationships and unity with your brothers and sisters in Christ in every way possible. I hope you are learning to see your sin struggles through the lens of the gospel, be it gossip, sexual immorality, gluttony, vanity, anger, bitterness, disobedience, or whatever. And may you be ready to do effective battle with Satan the moment you put this book down. God has accomplished much for you on the cross. Now go live in light of it all.

I Peter 2:24 He himself bore our sins in his body on the tree, that we might die to sin and live to righteousness. By his wounds you have been healed.

**We have by no means exhausted the wealth of all God has to say to us in Ephesians. If you are interested in further study, I recommend John Stott's *Message of Ephesians* or Martin Lloyd Jones' *Exposition of Ephesians*. Stott's is short and concise. Lloyd Jones' is much bigger (eight volumes to be precise) and goes into much more depth.

Final reflections

Discussion Questions

Introduction

1. As the opening paragraphs of the book asked, how do you think of yourself? Where do you look to find your identity? What are your insecurities?

2. Why are you studying this book? What do you hope to get out of this study?

3. What do you think God may have for you in this study?

Chapter 1

1. Has this chapter challenged your view of grace? In what ways?

2. How would you explain *peace through grace* to someone else?

Chapter 2

1. In an honest assessment of your daily life, does the reality of what is happening in the heavenly places influence how you view your earthly circumstances?

2. Think through both small and large struggles you are facing now. How do you view these struggles in light of Paul's words on our eternal reality in heaven?

Chapter 3

1. Explain in your own words what it means to be *in Christ*.

2. What are the implications of John 15:5 for your own life?

3. What does it look like in practical terms to make your thoughts submit to the truth?

Chapter 4

1. What are spiritual blessings?

2. How Does God's choosing of you and adopting you into his own family influence how you view yourself?

Chapter 5

1. What does Hosea's story teach you about your own story with God?

2. What is your inheritance in Christ? Does this inheritance influence how you view empty or lonely places in your life?

Chapter 6

1. In your own words what are the three things Paul prays we would know or understand in Ephesians 1: 15-23?

2. Have you had a time in your life when you realized after the fact that God worked in and through you with a power you could never have produced on your own?

Chapter 7

1. What was your spiritual situation apart from Christ?

2. Is it hard to hear that you by nature deserve God's wrath? Why or why not?

3. What do the words, "But God," in Ephesians 2:4 mean to you?

4. How does your spiritual inheritance equip you to face the struggles in your life this very day?

Chapter 8
1. Have you ever felt separated or alienated from God or his people? When and why?

2. Does your reality "now in Christ Jesus" address your answer to question 1? How?

3. Describe the access you now have to God through Christ. Do you take advantage of it?

Chapter 9
1. How does the contrast between a stranger and a fellow citizen inform how you view your place in the Body of Christ?

Chapter 11

1. Have you had a struggle in which, even if you were faithful to God, you could see no earthly value to your faithfulness?

2. Do Paul's words give you a different perspective on your suffering? If so, describe it.

Chapter 12

1. Does knowing Paul's earthly circumstances change how you read Ephesians 3: 14-20? If so, how?

Chapter 13

1. What manner of walking is worthy of the gospel of Christ?

2. Did any quality listed in Ephesians 4:2 stand out to you as being particularly relevant to situations you are facing? Why?

3. Can you think of a time when you witnessed a gentle reaction to conflict? What was the outcome?

4. Write out the I Corinthians 13 definition of love in your own words.

Chapter 14

1. Why must we pursue unity in the Body of Christ?

2. Have you experienced a situation in which people separated themselves from another group of Christians or individual Christian? Were the principles Paul set up here followed? Without getting into gossip, explain your thoughts.

Chapter 15

1. Before reading this chapter, what was your view of spiritual gifts?

2. Has your view changed? If so, in what ways?

Chapter 16
1. Explain *speaking the truth in love* in your own words.

2. Have you ever spoken truth without love? Have you loved without speaking truth? What were the results?

Chapter 17
1. Have you had times in your life characterized by futile though patters? What were the results?

2. The author said in the text that Christ is God's doctrinal statement. What does that sentence mean to you?

3. Where in your life is God moving you to put off old and put on new ways of dealing with issues?

Chapter 18
1. Have you experienced a time when you held on to anger or bitterness just to see Satan take opportunity to hurt you or another through it? What was the result?

Chapter 19
1. Think of a time someone ministered God's grace to you through his or her words. How did it influence you?

2. Have you experienced a situation in which the Spirit was quenched through inappropriate words?

Chapter 20
1. Define tenderhearted in your own words.

2. Think of a time someone responded to you with a tender heart. How did it minister to you?

3. How do you react when you read of the link between God's forgiveness of us and our forgiveness of others?

Chapter 21

1. Does the command to be imitators of God sound hard? How has God equipped you through Christ to do this?

2. Christ's example defines what it means to "walk in love." How would you summarize it to another?

Chapter 22

1. Does thanksgiving seem an odd replacement for sexual impurity? Why?

2. What is God's good view of sex? How do you embrace it as a married woman?
As a single woman?

Chapter 23
1. In your Christian culture, can a woman with a sexual history find support in her
journey from sin to reconciliation? If not, how can you foster an environment where
she can honestly confess her sin and struggle?

2. Have you experienced worldly sorrow over a sin issue? How did you feel? What
were your responses?

3. How would you counsel a friend who confessed a shameful sexual issue to you?

Chapter 25
1. Compare the exposure of sin apart from the gospel with the exposure of sin in light
of the gospel. What are the difference in the process and the results?

2. Is there sin in your life you need to expose to the light? If so are you ready to trust God and his gospel by doing so?

Chapter 26
1. What is the difference in being sealed with the Spirit and being filled with the Spirit?

2. The phrase, "submitting to one another out of reverence for Christ," is the summary of this section and the springboard for the next. Explain it in your own words.

Chapter 27
1. How does "submitting to one another out of reverence for Christ" inform the command for wives to submit to their own husbands?

2. Why is the call to submit to your own husband hard? How does your inheritance in Christ help you embrace it?

Chapter 28

1. How does the nature of Christ's profound love for you equip you to deal with situations where you do not feel loved on earth?

Chapter 29

1. Do you tense at the command to respect your husband? Why or why not?

2. Why is respect a valuable tool in Christian marriages?

Chapter 30

1. If you have a parent that is hard to honor, how do you apply Ephesians 6:2 in light of your inheritance in Christ?

2. How does God parent his children? How does that change how you should parent yours?

3. Even if you do not have children, what do you think of Paul's emphasis with parents (as he does with husbands and masters) of the restraint of authoritarian practices?

Chapter 31
1. Is Paul's teaching on slaves and masters relevant today? Why or why not?

Chapter 32
1. Have you had a situation in which you attacked a person thinking they were your enemy instead of a prisoner of your enemy? What was the outcome?

2. Are you sensitive to criticism? Why or why not?

3. Of the individual pieces of the armor of God, did one seem particularly relevant to the ways you have experienced Satan's attacks on you? In what way did it address your particular experience?

Chapter 33

1. Using the Hebrews 6 definition as a baseline, how would you define faith in your own words?

2. This chapter gave a particular example (the issue of sexual sin) of the truth of Scripture refuting the lies of Satan. What lies does Satan whisper to you about the sin issues with which you struggle? How does Scripture refute them?

Chapter 34

1. How does your prayer life compare with Paul's instructions in Ephesians 6:18? If there is a difference, why do you think that is?

Chapter 35

1. One of the opening discussion questions asked what you thought God might have for you in this study. As you look back on all Paul has taught on peace through grace throughout Ephesians, how would you answer that question now?

CPSIA information can be obtained at www.ICGtesting.com
235426LV00005B/50/P